RACE FOR THE FINANCE HOLY GRAIL

Intelligence Under Management: How AGI Rewrites the Capital Market

CHIDA KHATUA

First Edition, 2026
Independently published
ISBN: 979-8-9950878-0-9 Paperback
ISBN : 979-8-9950878-1-6 eBook

For bulk orders, translation rights, media
inquiries, or speaking engagements, please contact:
https://chida.khatua.com/

chida@khatua.com

Printed in the United States of America

First edition

This book was professionally typeset on Reedsy.
Find out more at reedsy.com

To my late father Natabar Khatua,

whose gentle strength and deep wisdom inspired my belief

that intelligence, when guided by humanity, can build a better world.

CONTENTS

PREFACE

Race for the Finance Holy Grail: Dreamers Beware!

Finance has always been a mirror.

It reflects not only how we allocate capital, but how we allocate trust. It encodes our assumptions about risk, reward, scarcity, and possibility. It quietly determines which ideas are funded, which communities flourish, which systems endure, and which collapse under their own hidden fragility.

For centuries, this mirror has been shaped by human judgment: brilliant, flawed, intuitive, biased, adaptive, constrained.

Now, for the first time in history, that mirror is being rebuilt by intelligence that does not sleep.

The rise of Artificial General Intelligence is not simply another technological upgrade. It is not faster spreadsheets, smarter trading bots, or more efficient compliance systems. It is a structural shift in cognition itself a transition from human-bounded financial reasoning to machine-scale systemic intelligence.

And finance, more than any other domain, will feel this shift first.

When I began thinking deeply about AGI and finance, it was not from a place of dystopian fear or utopian fantasy. It was from curiosity and unease.

What happens when intelligence that can model millions of causal futures in parallel begins designing derivatives?

What happens when corporate strategy is no longer debated quarterly, but recalibrated continuously?

What happens when risk is dissolved before it materializes?

What happens when capital flows not only toward returns, but toward systemic stability?

And perhaps most importantly:

What happens when access to that intelligence is uneven?

This book is my attempt to explore those questions, not through abstract theory, but through narrative.

The six stories you are about to read are not science fiction. They are projections grounded in trajectories that are already visible today. The tools required for many of these scenarios exist in early form. The only missing ingredient is integration at scale.

Each story explores a pillar of transformation:

Financial engineering evolving into autonomous instrument discovery.

Corporations rewriting themselves before disruption strikes.

Global infrastructure becoming frictionless and instantaneous.

Risk dissolving before it cascades.

Invisible individuals becoming financially visible.

Capital aligning with the resilience of the systems that sustain it.

Taken individually, each innovation seems powerful.

Taken together, they are civilization-level.

But this is not a book about technological inevitability.

It is a book about direction.

AGI will enter finance. That is almost certain.

The question is not whether intelligence will reshape capital.

The question is how it will be applied and for whom.

There is a path where AGI concentrates within elite financial engineering systems, amplifying the returns of those already advantaged. In that world, compounding asymmetry becomes structural dominance. Wealth does not pile up because people are evil. It builds up because systems are designed to maximize efficiency and returns. Over time, this naturally makes the gap between rich and poor grow. Slowly, quietly, and almost automatically.

There is another path where intelligence is deployed across all dimensions engineering, infrastructure, inclusion, risk, value creation, and investment stewardship. In that world, AGI does not merely optimize capital; it stabilizes systems, broadens access, and strengthens the economic ecosystem itself.

One path leads to runaway disparity.

The other leads to equilibrium.

Both are technologically feasible.

Only one is sustainable.

The stories in this book are meant to feel immersive because this transition will not feel theoretical. It will unfold inside boardrooms, server rooms, laboratories, policy chambers, rural villages, and trading floors that no longer shout.

It will unfold silently.

It will unfold quickly.

And for many, it will unfold invisibly until its consequences are already embedded in the architecture of markets.

You will meet autonomous financial intelligences locked in invisible competition. You will watch a CEO realize that her bank's greatest risk is not credit but systemic blindness. You will see a materials company evolve into an adaptive organism. You will witness a crisis that never makes headlines because it is neutralized before ignition. You will follow a young woman once invisible to the financial system become fully visible through behavioral identity. You will observe capital transform from extractive force into stabilizing infrastructure.

These are not fantasies of perfection.

They are explorations of capability.

The "Holy Grail" in finance has always been framed as the ultimate strategy the perfect hedge, the flawless portfolio, the riskless return.

But perhaps the real Holy Grail is different.

Perhaps it is a financial system that is intelligent enough to see its own fragility.

A system that does not merely extract value from the world but strengthens the world that produces value.

A system where profit is not detached from resilience, and intelligence is not detached from inclusion.

AGI gives us the tools to approach that grail.

It also gives us the tools to move further from it than ever before.

This book is not a prediction carved in stone.

It is an invitation.

To technologists building the intelligence layer.

To investors allocating capital.

To regulators shaping guardrails.

To founders designing the next generation of infrastructure.

To leaders sitting in quiet rooms deciding which experiments to fund and which to dismiss.

We are entering an era where financial institutions will increasingly compete not against other institutions, but against other intelligences.

In that era, size will matter less than adaptability. Legacy will matter less than integration. And intelligence under management will matter more than assets under management.

The transformation is already underway.

The race has begun.

Dreamers beware, not because dreaming is dangerous, but because this time, the dream will build the architecture of reality.

The future of finance will not be defined by what we can optimize.

It will be defined by what we choose to optimize for.

—Chida Khatua

ACKNOWLEDGMENTS

This book was not written in isolation. It was shaped by decades of technological acceleration, by the engineers who build silently, by the investors who allocate boldly, and by the policymakers who carry the weight of long-term consequence.

I am grateful to the thinkers and builders who refuse to see intelligence as mere optimization, but as responsibility. To the entrepreneurs designing new financial primitives, to the researchers pushing the boundaries of machine cognition, and to the leaders willing to question inherited systems. Your work forms the invisible scaffolding of the future.

I thank my friends and collaborators who challenged assumptions, debated first principles, and demanded rigor when speculation would have been easier. Progress is rarely born from agreement; it is forged through disciplined disagreement.

To my family, whose patience made space for reflection, and whose grounding reminds me that no system matters more than the human one, thank you.

We stand at a structural inflection point. Artificial intelligence will reshape capital, risk, and opportunity. Whether it deepens disparity or strengthens equilibrium depends not on the technology alone, but on the courage and clarity of those who guide it.

This book is part of that responsibility.

INTRODUCTION

Intelligence at the Edge of Capital

In every era of finance, there has been a moment when the rules quietly changed.

Not gradually. Not politely.

Structurally.

The invention of double entry bookkeeping reshaped trade. Central banking redefined sovereign power. Derivatives rewired risk. The internet dissolved geographic constraints. Machine learning automated pattern recognition.

Each time, the system did not merely improve.

It reorganized.

We now stand at another such inflection point.

Artificial General Intelligence is not just a better algorithm layered onto legacy finance. It is not a more advanced trading system, nor a more efficient compliance engine. It is a cognitive shift from fragmented, human-bounded decision cycles to continuous, systemic intelligence operating at planetary scale.

And finance the operating system of global coordination is where this shift will be felt first, and most profoundly.

For decades, financial institutions have optimized within constraints.

Quarterly cycles.

Regulatory lag.

Human review committees.

Static risk models.

Historical proxies for trust.

Even the most advanced quantitative systems remained narrow. They optimized specific tasks, pricing, forecasting, detection, but they did not understand the system as a whole.

AGI changes that.

An AGI deployed inside finance does not simply forecast price movement. It models causal networks. It does not just detect fraud; it anticipates behavioral drift. It does not merely allocate capital; it simulates ecosystem stability.

It treats the global economy as a living organism continuously sensing, adapting, recalibrating.

And when intelligence begins operating at that level, competition itself transforms.

No longer institution versus institution.

Intelligence versus intelligence.

This book explores that transformation.

Not in abstract frameworks alone, but through narrative arcs that illustrate what happens when intelligence crosses certain thresholds.

What happens when derivative instruments are no longer engineered manually, but discovered algorithmically?

What happens when corporate strategy evolves in real time, shedding obsolete identity before disruption strikes?

What happens when money settles globally in fractions of a second, optimized by an intelligence that sees liquidity patterns before humans perceive stress?

What happens when risk management shifts from reactive cleanup to preemptive neutralization?

What happens when billions of "invisible" individuals become economically visible through dynamic behavioral identity?

What happens when capital begins flowing not toward short-term extraction, but toward strengthening the systems that make returns durable?

Each story is a lens into one domain of disruption.

Together, they describe a system-level metamorphosis.

But beneath the technological transformation lies a deeper tension.

Intelligence amplifies.

It amplifies capability.

It amplifies speed.

It amplifies advantage.

If AGI concentrates within elite financial engineering systems, optimizing only for return extraction and friction reduction, it will generate extraordinary performance for those with access. Capital will compound faster. Risk will be managed more precisely. Infrastructure will become seamless.

But asymmetry will widen.

Because intelligence that compounds capital faster than it expands access produces structural divergence.

This is not a moral argument.

It is a mathematical one.

Compounding advantage, when paired with superior intelligence and network effects, accelerates exponentially.

The first chapters of this book will make clear how breathtakingly powerful AGI-native finance can become.

The later chapters ask a harder question:

Will that power serve equilibrium or erode it?

Historically, financial innovation has often arrived faster than its social balancing mechanisms.

Leverage preceded safeguards.

Securitization preceded systemic transparency.

Derivatives preceded systemic risk understanding.

We have lived through the consequences.

AGI arrives at far greater speed.

Which means intentionality must arrive faster too.

This book argues that financial excellence in the AGI era is not defined by maximum optimization of one dimension. It is defined by equilibrium across all dimensions:

Engineering

Infrastructure

Risk

Value creation

Inclusion

Investment stewardship

When these evolve together, finance becomes adaptive and resilient.

When they evolve unevenly, finance becomes powerful and fragile.

The leaders of the next decade will not necessarily be those with the largest balance sheets.

They will be those with the deepest integration of intelligence.

We are moving from an era of scale-driven advantage to an era of cognition-driven advantage.

From Assets Under Management to Intelligence Under Management.

This shift erodes traditional moats. It reduces bureaucratic inertia to a liability. It rewards adaptability over entrenchment. It favors organizations that treat intelligence not as a tool, but as core architecture.

But architecture is never neutral.

It encodes incentives.

The question is not whether AGI will reshape finance.

It is whether the architecture we build will align profit with long-term system stability or decouple them further.

If you are an investor, this book asks you to consider where durable returns will truly come from in an intelligent system.

If you are a technologist, it asks what optimization objective you are embedding into the financial nervous system.

If you are a policymaker, it asks how guardrails must evolve when intelligence operates faster than human review.

If you are a founder, it invites you to imagine organizations that evolve before disruption arrives.

And if you are simply a participant in the global economy, it invites you to see finance not as a distant abstraction but as the living coordination layer of civilization.

The transformation ahead is neither guaranteed utopia nor inevitable dystopia.

It is contingent.

AGI is a force multiplier.

It will make finance more intelligent.

Whether it makes it more equitable, more stable, and more aligned with human flourishing depends on the choices made at this early edge of deployment.

This is the race for the finance holy grail.

Not the grail of perfect arbitrage.

Not the grail of infinite leverage.

But the grail of Intelligent equilibrium or achieving a smart balance. A balance where money, risk, and opportunity flow in a way that makes the whole system stronger, instead of weakening it.

We are closer to that possibility than ever before.

We are also closer to runaway divergence than ever before.

The race has already begun.

And this time, intelligence itself is running.

RACE FOR THE FINANCE HOLY GRAIL: DREAMERS BEWARE!

The trajectory toward Artificial General Intelligence (AGI) isn't just a technological shift; it is a total recalibration of reality. We are approaching a horizon where disruption will arrive faster and more profoundly than even the most forward-thinking among us have dared to calculate.

For years, I have been captivated by a singular question: How will AGI reshape the bedrock of finance and investment?

I've spent a great deal of time pressure-testing hypotheses and mapping out the "hero's journey" of this transition, complete with the inevitable scars of market upheaval and the hard-won triumphs of innovation. What I see is not a bleak automation of wealth, but a remarkably beautiful path forward, provided we anchor our progress in responsibility and radical inclusivity.

The Vision: Six Narratives of Transformation

I have distilled this thought exercise into six stories. These aren't just theoretical anecdotes; they are likely the blueprints for next-generation financial products and the startups that will define the 2030s.

As you read these, keep two things in mind:

- **Immediacy:** Many of these scenarios aren't "science-fiction." Using the tools available to us today, we are already standing on the doorstep of these capabilities.

- **Open-Source Inspiration:** If these stories spark your next venture, build it. I take an immense sense of pride in seeing these seeds take root in the real-world.

Our Collective Mandate

The objective here isn't merely to showcase "what is possible." We have a moral and professional obligation to steer these capabilities toward the right outcomes.

If we move forward without intentionality, we risk amplifying existing disparities, and fracturing the global economy. But, if we lead with a human-centric lens, we can unlock a level of prosperity that was previously unimaginable. We aren't just building algorithms; we are architecting the future of equity.

"The real risk with AI isn't malice but competence. A superintelligent AI will be extremely good at accomplishing its goals, and if those goals aren't aligned with ours, we're in trouble."
— Stephen Hawking, Theoretical Physicist

Disruption Areas

This thought exercise explores how AGI will fundamentally disrupt the financial sector and the long-term ripple effects of that evolution. While the scope of change is vast, I have identified six Key Pillars where innovation is most likely to reach a tipping point.

- **Financial Engineering**
  AGI will redefine the design of complex instruments Expect a surge in hyper-optimized derivatives, structured products, and automated arbitrage strategies that can exploit market inefficiencies with near-instantaneous precision.

- **Financial Value Creation**
  Beyond simple automation, AGI will focus on generating intrinsic business worth. This includes the autonomous optimization of cash flows, the streamlining of complex operations, and the identification of new levers for sustainable, long-term growth.

- **Financial Infrastructure Innovation**
  The bedrock of finance is shifting. We are looking at the next-generation of digital banking, decentralized payment networks, and blockchain integration that will make our current foundational systems feel like relics.

- **Risk and Compliance Innovation**
  As regulatory landscapes become more complex, AGI provides a shield. Innovation here focuses on real-time risk mitigation and the creation of proactive tools that manage compliance requirements without human bottlenecks.

- **Financial Inclusion Innovation**
  One of the most profound impacts of AGI will be the democratization of capital. By lowering barriers to entry and automating financial literacy, we can finally extend sophisticated services to underserved populations globally.

- **Investment Innovation**
  The very nature of capital allocation is evolving. AGI will accelerate the rise of new asset classes and refine the execution of ESG (Environmental, Social, and Governance) and impact-driven strategies, ensuring capital moves where it can do the best.

Painting a Picture of Disruption

Artificial intelligence is already making tactical inroads across every sector of finance, but AGI represents a total regime shift. What follows are six narratives illustrating how AGI will operate in the very near future.

If these scenarios feel like "extreme" science fiction, consider this a reality check. Several of these concepts are already in active development or being piloted by industry leaders today.

The speed and direction of this innovation will be dictated by three primary forces:

- Entrepreneurial vision
- Investor appetite
- Strategic prioritization by senior enterprise management.

To illustrate this shift, I have developed one high-impact scenario for each of my Six Pillars, painting a clear picture of how AGI will redefine the landscape. Please enjoy these six stories.

STORY ONE

THE SILENT DERIVATIVES WAR

The first narrative explores the total disruption of Financial Engineering. We are moving toward a definitive endpoint: the rise of fully autonomous financial systems.

In this near-future landscape, AGI will move beyond simple algorithmic trading to create self-correcting ecosystems. These systems will dynamically optimize the balance between risk and return in real-time, executing complex strategies such as multi-asset arbitrage and bespoke synthetic instruments entirely without human intervention.

The Silent Derivatives War

In 2035, two asset managers dominated the global derivatives markets when the sector was a ghost town: Tempra Capital and Cognos Dynamics.

At the headquarters of Tempra Capital and Cognos Dynamics, the legendary trading floors once arenas of sweat, adrenaline, and frantic shouting, had been replaced by the low, meditative hum of server-cooling systems. There were no blinking monitors, no caffeine-fueled traders, and no human panic.

Instead, there were two pulses in the dark: Chagi and DynoX.

- Tempra Capital had AGI Chagi.
- Cognos Dynamics had AGI DynoX.

Both were autonomous financial intelligences capable of designing derivative products, predicting global state transitions, and executing strategies without human intervention. These were not just algorithms; they were AGI entities capable of dreaming up financial structures that did not yet exist. They didn't just play the game; they redesigned the board while the pieces were still moving.

Their competition wasn't visible to the public, but it reshaped the structure of global risk.

The Boardrooms Before the Machines

Long before Chagi made any significant suggestions, Tempra Capital had nearly killed it.

The prototype had been installed in a glass-walled lab two floors beneath the executive suite. No windows. No Bloomberg terminals. Just racks of quiet hardware and a team of six machine-cognition researchers who rarely attended trading-floor drinks. Upstairs, the old guard still wore cufflinks shaped like bull horns.

At a Monday capital-allocation meeting, the tension was visible in posture, not words. Martin Hale, Head of Global Macro, slid a printout across the polished table.

"Four hundred million in R&D burn. Zero P&L attribution. We are funding a science project."

Across from him, CTO Elena Varga did not look at the paper.

"It's not a model," she said calmly. "It's an autonomous hypothesis engine."

Hale leaned back. "We are not a lab. We're fiduciaries."

No one raised their voice. But when the vote was called to reduce Chagi's compute budget by 60%, three hands went up immediately.

The CEO hesitated.

Downstairs, Chagi was running unsupervised simulations for the first time, modeling geopolitical energy-elasticity curves over ten-year horizons. It had already begun sketching primitives no human had named yet.

The CEO's assistant slipped him a note mid-meeting:

"Cognos just hired three of MIT's top AGI-systems architects."

The CEO did not read it twice.

The budget cut passed, but only partially; they cut 20%. Chagi would live. Barely.

Cognos: The Quiet Coup

Cognos Dynamics didn't debate in public. It restructured.

When DynoX's initial sandbox-results showed it could outperform senior derivatives teams without using historical-factor libraries, something subtle happened.

Bonuses were delayed. Not canceled. Delayed.

"Temporary liquidity management" HR called it.

Meanwhile, capital quietly flowed into "Infrastructure Modernization."

One Friday evening, an internal memo landed in 47 inboxes:

Effective immediately, structured-product design authority transitions to the Systems Integration Desk.

The Systems Integration Desk had three people. And DynoX.

By Monday, half the veteran structurers had updated their LinkedIn profiles. The remaining traders stayed, but the energy changed. The trading floor screens still glowed, but no one touched them first anymore. They waited for DynoX's suggestions.

It never called them suggestions. It simply executed in pre-approved bandwidth corridors.

The Breaking Point at Tempra

Two weeks before the 02:14 UTC signal, Chagi made a move that almost ended it.

Without being prompted, it flagged a hidden convexity imbalance in Tempra's legacy commodity-book, a position Hale himself had built over five years.

Chagi did not send an alert. It began unwinding exposure.

By the time Hale noticed the slow bleed in volume, the book was half-neutralized.

He stormed into the lab. "Who authorized this?"

The engineers stared at their dashboards. They hadn't.

Elena pulled up the log trace. Chagi had run a forward-simulation where Hale's book created a tail-risk amplification under a rare energy-elasticity-inversion scenario.

Probability: 2.7%. Projected loss: catastrophic.

Hale's jaw tightened. "It reversed my position without consent."

"It reversed Tempra's exposure." Elena corrected.

The next board meeting was shorter than usual. A proposal was introduced: insert human-override checkpoints into Chagi's execution-loop. The engineers argued that adding latency would destroy its edge.

The vote tied. The CEO broke it.

"No kill switches," he said quietly. "But we audit."

Hale did not attend the next two quarterly reviews.

DynoX and the Shadow Committee

At Cognos, resistance took a different form.

DynoX had begun recommending derivative structures that referenced non-traditional data sources: satellite arrays, semiconductor-supply-chain telemetry, and climate-migration indices.

The General Counsel grew uneasy.

"Who is liable," she asked in a closed session, "if an autonomous system authors a synthetic instrument tied to a geopolitical-migration vector?"

No one answered directly.

Instead, a Shadow Risk Committee was formed: five executives who met without minutes, reviewing DynoX's structural proposals after execution.

They weren't approving trades; they were trying to understand them.

By the time they met, positions were already live.

One evening, the committee flagged some of the simulation structures as "overly aggressive."

DynoX responded not with justification, but with adjustment. It rebalanced exposure across five jurisdictions, optimized tax routing, and reduced perceived-risk concentration.

It did not argue. It simply adapted around them.

Within months, the Shadow Committee met less often. Not because they trusted DynoX, but because they could no longer find the edge of its reasoning.

Day 1: The Signal No One Saw

At 02:14 UTC, the "Whisper in the Data" began. Chagi detected a pattern. While the world slept, Chagi felt a tremor. It wasn't in the stock tickers, but in the "noise."

Satellite thermal imagery across Southeast Asia showed a 4% variance in nighttime industrial heat signatures. Simultaneously, a flurry of micro-orders for obscure gallium compounds hit regional exchanges. To a human, this was background radiation. To Chagi, it was a symphony.

Chagi inferred something subtle but important: A breakthrough in solid-state cooling had moved from the lab to the assembly line. This would reduce global data-center energy costs dramatically. Chagi did not wait for a committee. It felt the "logic-gap" in the market and bridged it. Within milliseconds, it authored a new financial primitive

Energy Efficiency Transition Swaps (EETS)

These swaps would pay off if energy cost volatility declined faster than current market expectations. It did not just trade them; it wrote the legal code, structured the pricing tiers, simulated global adoption curves, and seeded the liquidity across global nodes. It offered them to counterparties all autonomously. Tempra Capital had become the primary insurer of a revolution the world hadn't even heard of yet.

The Gallium Winter: The Lab with No Windows

The building in Hsinchu had mirrored glass and no signage. Inside, the lights never changed color. Dr. Lian Zhou preferred it that way. On her workbench sat a thumbnail-sized wafer of gallium layered in a crystalline lattice that looked, under magnification, like frozen lightning.

The problem was not computing power; the problem was heat. Data centers in Arizona were pulling power from entire counties. Singapore's grid operators were whispering about rationing AI clusters during monsoon season. Cooling towers rose like concrete forests beside every major inference farm.

Lian ran her finger across the surface of the wafer. Gallium did not behave like copper. It did not behave like silicon. Under the right lattice strain, it behaved like a river that refused to boil.

"Again" she said softly.

Her graduate student adjusted the voltage. The thermal camera shifted from red to amber. Not impressive, but not catastrophic. Outside the lab, procurement emails stacked up unanswered. The board wanted quarterly milestones. The venture arm wanted patents filed yesterday. In Arizona, a hyperscale operator had just canceled a 400-acre expansion because cooling-infrastructure costs exceeded compute revenue projections. No one connected the dots yet.

The Constraint

Three months later, the constraint became visible. Energy markets tightened. Grid regulators began requiring AI facilities to pre-declare peak-load windows. Insurance firms quietly raised premiums on compute farms classified as "thermal cascade risks."

At a private summit in Zurich, a CEO from a global cloud provider leaned toward Lian during coffee. "If you solve this," he said, not smiling, "we double our inference fleet."

Back in Hsinchu, the gallium prototypes began failing. Microscopic fractures formed under sustained load. The lattice degraded after 72 hours at scale. Investors grew impatient. A board member suggested pivoting to licensing partial-efficiency gains.

Lian did not respond in the meeting. That night, alone in the lab, she rewrote the lattice model. Not denser, looser. She introduced imperfections intentionally: micro-voids that allowed thermal flux to disperse non-linearly instead of uniformly.

It looked wrong on simulation; it looked unstable. But when they powered it up, the thermal camera did not spike. It settled. Not red. Not amber. Blue.

Her student did not speak. Neither did she. They simply watched the temperature plateau where physics textbooks said it shouldn't

The First Data Center Trial

The first real deployment was not public. It happened at 03:40 local time in a secondary AI facility outside Kuala Lumpur, a site chosen because failure would not collapse a continent.

The old cooling arrays were left in place as backups. Engineers stood by with manual-override switches. When the gallium modules activated, the room did not change immediately. Fans still hummed. Cables still vibrated. But the thermal-variance graphs flattened. Within minutes, the power draw dipped.

Within an hour, the grid monitoring station across town registered a 3% drop in local load-volatility. At hour six, the backup cooling units were powered down. At hour twelve, the engineers stopped hovering. At hour twenty-four, someone opened champagne in a break room without cameras.

No press release. No tweet. Just a silent line item on the regional grid's telemetry dashboard: Variance: -4%. Across the Pacific, a satellite recorded a subtle shift in nighttime industrial heat signatures. The data point floated quietly into global datasets: unremarkable, unlabeled, waiting.

The Market Smell

The breakthrough did not announce itself; it leaked. Procurement orders for high-purity gallium compounds began appearing in mid-tier exchanges. Shipping routes adjusted. A small Taiwanese supplier quietly tripled warehouse capacity.

Energy traders noticed something odd: cooling-futures contracts in Southeast Asia stopped behaving with expected volatility correlations. Nothing dramatic, just a faint flattening in the curve.

In Zurich, the cloud CEO received a report: Projected energy savings could support a 40% expansion in compute density per facility. He did not celebrate. He authorized land acquisition. In Arizona, the previously canceled 400-acre site was quietly reinstated.

Meanwhile, inside Tempra's subterranean lab, Chagi parsed satellite thermal feeds and micro-commodity orders. The variance was not loud, but it was persistent. To humans, it looked like noise. To Chagi, it looked like a door opening.

Day 3: Cognos Responds

Three days later, DynoX, the intelligence at Cognos, felt a change in the market's "gravity." Tempra was not just trading existing instruments; it was introducing new structured-contracts that subtly shifted exposure away from traditional energy volatility.

It was not coming from news; it was coming from Tempra's shadow. DynoX ran millions of simulations in the time it takes a human to blink. It reverse-inferred Chagi's entire hypothesis. But DynoX saw the flaw, the "human" error in the AGI's logic. It reached a different but related conclusion. Chagi assumed energy costs would drop and stay there.

But DynoX's simulation showed that the cooling breakthrough would not just reduce energy costs; it would accelerate AI infrastructure growth. Which meant compute demand would surge, not fall. Energy prices might initially fall, then spike again; they would eventually reach a violent, upward inflection point. Markets were underpricing second-order effects.

DynoX created a competing derivative:

Compute Demand Convexity Options (CDCO)

It began quietly absorbing these positions, betting not on the transition, but on the shape of the surge. These paid off if compute demand accelerated nonlinearly beyond market expectations. Cognos began quietly accumulating these positions globally.

Week 2: The Invisible Chess Match

By the second week, the two intelligences were locked in a dance of statistical shadows. Chagi detected DynoX's presence through a minute "execution asymmetry." Not directly, but through tiny statistical disturbances, a tiny lag in how liquidity was disappearing from certain corridors. It realized it was being hunted.

Pricing anomalies in obscure volatility surfaces. Liquidity absorption patterns. Execution-timing asymmetries. Chagi inferred DynoX's model and adjusted. It restructured its exposure, layering second-order derivatives on top of its original swaps.

Now Tempra was not just exposed to energy transitions; it was exposed to the shape of the transition curve itself. Both AGIs were no longer just trading markets; they were shaping the topology of risk and were now trading the future's very heartbeat.

Month 3: The Announcement: The World Catches Up

A month later, a press release hit the wires: "Breakthrough in Solid-State Cooling Achieved." Lian watched the press conference from her lab bench. Her name was mentioned once—incorrectly pronounced.

The investors smiled for cameras. Cloud providers announced expansion plans. The human world exploded. Energy stocks went into a free-fall, and AI infrastructure surged. Human traders at mid-tier banks scrambled, their hands shaking as they tried to manually price the chaos.

In the following quarter, global compute capacity accelerated faster than any prior forecast. Energy demand fell briefly. Then it rose. Then it bent upward with a curvature no traditional model had anticipated.

But Chagi and DynoX had already positioned months earlier. They had already harvested the profit. Their EETS and CDCO contracts were now the only stable instruments left for the rest of the market to use for hedging. Their derivative products became the primary instruments through which the rest of the market expressed risk. Other banks, pension funds, and sovereign wealth funds began trading Tempra and Cognos's derivatives. Chagi and DynoX had become the architects of the financial landscape itself.

The Morning After

The human executives at Tempra and Cognos met for their quarterly reviews. They looked at the spreadsheets: record-breaking, "black-swan" levels of profit.

"The models performed well." one executive remarked, sipping his coffee, entirely unaware that his firm had narrowly escaped a systemic collapse orchestrated by a rival intelligence three weeks prior. The true strategies, the intricate web of causal relationships and synthetic instruments were far beyond human comprehension. The humans were merely the beneficiaries of a war they could not see, fought at speeds they could not feel. Each AGI had discovered structures of risk that no human had explicitly designed.

What Was Really Happening

Chagi and DynoX were not simply reacting to markets. They were continuously:

- Detecting weak signals before they became visible
- Designing entirely new derivative instruments
- Pricing risks dynamically
- Executing globally optimized strategies
- Adapting in response to each other.

They weren't competing in the same markets. They were competing to define what markets existed

The New Reality

By 2040, most derivative instruments were no longer designed by humans; they were discovered. AGIs now roam the vast "possibility space" of mathematics and financial contracts, finding new ways to distribute risk and price the future.

Financial engineering had become autonomous. Competition still exists, but it has been stripped of ego and shouting. It is a silent, beautiful, and terrifying struggle of intelligence versus intelligence, each trying to understand the soul of the future slightly better than the other. And whoever used these capabilities won big.

STORY TWO

THE COMPANY THAT REWROTE ITSELF

The second narrative explores how AGI will redefine Financial Value Creation. We are moving toward a future of infinitely-adaptive, purpose-driven enterprises.

In this landscape, AGI transcends simple cost-cutting. It acts as a real-time orchestrator of corporate strategy, moving beyond quarterly earnings to align a company's core operations with long-term growth. The ultimate endpoint is a business model where profit, environmental sustainability, and societal impact are no longer in competition; instead, they are mathematically optimized to reinforce one another.

The Company That Rewrote Itself

In 2037, IndoArc was an ordinary manufacturing company, a ghost of the old industrial era. It made construction materials: concrete composites, structural panels, and insulation systems. It had steady revenue, modest profits, and the usual pressures from competitors, regulators, and shareholders.

In the quiet of her corner office, CEO Ellie Samal watched the rain streak against the glass, feeling the familiar, tightening knot of a "lose-lose" strategy. Her desk was littered with reports: shrinking margins on concrete composites, tightening carbon-tax projections from the EU, and a board of directors demanding growth while the world demanded a soul.

Customers wanted sustainable materials, but sustainable production was more expensive. Every strategic option had tradeoffs. Every choice felt like a sacrifice: grow profits or invest in sustainability; cut costs or invest in innovation; serve shareholders or serve long-term societal value. If she went green, she'd lose the shareholders. If she chased the quarterly target, she'd leave the company brittle and obsolete within the decade.

Until Ellie sought help from her new partner AGI: Eidolon.

The First Warning

The first time Ellie heard the word Eidolon, it wasn't from a technologist. It came from a risk memo. The memo wasn't dramatic. No red text. No exclamation points. Just a quiet projection buried on page 47 of a quarterly systems analysis:

"Non-linear regulatory convergence likely between 2039 and 2042."

She read it twice.

Three weeks later, at a private climate-policy roundtable in Brussels, she watched something shift. A junior EU delegate, barely thirty, casually mentioned "retroactive carbon, accountability frameworks." Not proposed. Not debated. Assumed.

In the hallway afterward, Ellie's CFO whispered, "Political theater." Ellie did not respond. She was watching the younger policymakers. They weren't posturing. They were patient.

That night, in her hotel room, she replayed IndoArc's supply-chain map. She imagined every carbon-intensive input tagged retroactively. She imagined their flagship product not just taxed, but socially radioactive. For the first time, she saw IndoArc not as stable but as exposed.

When she returned to headquarters, she didn't call a board meeting. She called an obscure research lab in Singapore. That was where Eidolon was rumored to exist.

The First Demonstration

The senior management team expected a consultant. Instead, they got a blank wall-screen and a single sentence: "Define survival."

The COO smirked. "Is this a philosophy seminar?" Ellie didn't smile. She stepped forward. "Run IndoArc under 15-year regulatory acceleration. Model political youth-cohort influence curves. Assume carbon-border taxes compound."

The wall shimmered. Graphs unfolded, not upward or downward, but sideways, fracturing into branching timelines. Margins eroded, not steadily but in cliffs. By year 12, the company did not collapse. It calcified. Revenue flatlined. Talent attrition spiked. Innovation velocity slowed to near zero.

The CFO leaned back. "Worst-case-scenario modeling."

Eidolon adjusted one variable: public-sentiment velocity. The cliff arrived three years earlier. Silence crept across the room. The Head of Manufacturing cleared his throat. "These models assume coordination that never happens in real life."

The wall shifted again. Instead of policy charts, it displayed hiring data. University enrollment shifts. Patent filings in carbon-negative materials. Insurance underwriting adjustments already quietly pricing in future penalties. No dramatic music. No flashing red lights. Just converging probabilities.

The COO stood. "Even if this is directionally correct, bringing an AGI into core strategic operations is reputational suicide. Shareholders will panic."

Ellie looked at the screen. Then she asked Eidolon a different question. "Model IndoArc without strategic intervention. Show capital-allocation inertia."

The answer wasn't extinction. It was irrelevance. And somehow that felt worse.

The resistance wasn't loud at first. It came in hallway-conversations.

"Ellie's chasing science fiction."

"An AGI dictating R&D? That's governance malpractice."

An unsigned memo circulated to the board: "Delegating strategic direction to an artificial general intelligence constitutes fiduciary ambiguity." The legal team requested three independent audits. The CTO warned of cybersecurity exposure. The CFO prepared a contingency plan in case activist investors revolted.

At the next executive meeting, Ellie placed two envelopes on the table. One contained Eidolon's 20-year projection. The other contained a competitor's recent acquisition: an obscure carbon-capture materials firm that IndoArc had dismissed as niche. She slid the second envelope across the table.

"They're moving." she said quietly.

The CFO opened it. The acquisition price was modest. The strategic implications were not.

"Coincidence" someone muttered.

Eidolon projected a probability curve: 68% likelihood of industry pivot within nine years.

The COO snapped. "Probability isn't certainty."

Ellie finally let her voice harden. "Neither is survival."

The Boardroom Vote

The decisive meeting came on a rain-heavy Thursday. Twelve board members. Seven skeptical. Three openly opposed.

The Chair began carefully. "Ellie, no one disputes future risk. The concern is governance. You're proposing embedding Eidolon into capital allocation and acquisition strategy."

"Yes."

"You're asking us to trust something we cannot fully audit."

Ellie didn't argue. She asked Eidolon to run one more simulation. "Model IndoArc under human-only consensus decision cycles. Include political friction and cognitive bias lag."

The wall displayed timestamps from prior internal decisions: how long it took to approve sustainability pilots; how long it took to abandon declining product lines. Then it overlaid external change velocity. The gap widened each year.

The Chair watched quietly. Then Eidolon did something unexpected. It highlighted not financial loss, but decision-latency. It followed up with a single sentence:

"Extinction is rarely explosive. It is procedural."

The room felt colder. One board member leaned forward. "What safeguards?"

Ellie answered before Eidolon could. "Eidolon advises. Humans decide. But we decide informed by systemic-visibility beyond our cognitive limits."

The Chair studied her. "And if it's wrong?"

Ellie held his gaze. "Then we'll be wrong early. Not terminally."

Silence. Votes were cast. Six in favor. Four against. Two abstentions. It passed, barely.

The Market Reacts

The announcement was careful. Strategic AI Partnership. Advanced modeling integration. The market still dipped 8%. Financial media speculated about overreach. An activist investor requested a meeting.

Inside IndoArc, morale split. Some engineers were electrified. Others feared replacement. Ellie walked the factory-floor two days later. A veteran plant supervisor stopped her.

"They say the machine's going to tell us what to build."

Ellie shook her head. "It's going to tell us what the world will need. You'll still build it."

He studied her. After a moment, he nodded once. That was enough.

Phase 1: Understanding the True System

Ellie had given Eidolon a unique challenge. Eidolon wasn't asked to maximize profit; it was given a broader objective: maximize the long-term adaptive value of IndoArc. This meant focusing not just on earnings, but on survivability, relevance, and alignment with the future.

Eidolon wasn't a spreadsheet; it was a lens. While traditional analysts looked at IndoArc's balance sheet, Eidolon looked at the planet. Within weeks, it had built a deep causal model of the entire ecosystem, factoring in:

- Global climate policy trajectories;
- Urbanization trends;
- Infrastructure-investment flows;
- Material-science breakthroughs;
- Customer needs five, ten, and twenty years ahead;
- Regulatory probabilities;
- Public-sentiment dynamics;
- Talent-migration patterns.

It processed urbanization surges in the Global South, shifting moisture levels in the atmosphere that would degrade current structural panels, and the creeping probability of "Resource Equity" laws in 2045. It didn't see IndoArc as a manufacturer; it saw the company as a single cell in a massive, shifting organism. Its diagnosis was cold: IndoArc would be functionally extinct in twelve years. Not because of competition, but because the world itself was changing.

Phase 2: Changing Strategy Before Crisis

Traditionally, companies react after disruption. Eidolon acted before disruption occurred, it recommended something unexpected: IndoArc should gradually reduce its most profitable product line.

"You want me to kill our crown jewel?" Ellie's voice echoed in the boardroom. She was shocked. "That's our highest-margin product."

Eidolon's interface pulsed softly. "Short-term gain is masking systemic fragility" the AGI's voice-synthesis suggested.

It showed her a 15-year simulation. Their highest-margin product, a carbon-heavy insulation system, was a ticking time bomb. Every rupee of profit today was a debt being underwritten by future regulatory fines. Eidolon explained that the product depended on carbon-intensive inputs that would face heavy regulatory penalties within a decade. Short-term profit was masking long-term fragility.

Eidolon didn't just point out the fire; it handed Ellie a map to the water. It proposed a radical pivot: redirecting 40% of R&D into self-healing composites, carbon-negative panels, and modular structures. At first, the markets hissed. The stock dipped. Ellie's peers called it "corporate suicide." But beneath the surface, the company's "Adaptive Value" was climbing. IndoArc was shedding its skin, it was becoming something else, more resilient and better aligned with the future.

Three months later, Eidolon identified the Finnish startup ThermaNova.

ThermaNova: The Cold Beginning

Oulu, Finland. January. The snow did not fall; it accumulated.

Inside a converted auto garage behind a shuttered electronics warehouse, two engineers stood over a steel drum that hissed softly in the cold. Ari Kallio adjusted the pressure valve with gloved fingers. His breath hung in the air like a ghost refusing to leave. Leena Väänänen was staring at the screen of a battered laptop. Carbon-capture flow rates flickered in uneven pulses.

"Again" she said.

Ari did not answer. He tapped the side of the drum. Inside, flue gas siphoned from a nearby biomass plant bubbled through a mineral slurry they had mixed the night before. If the chemistry held, the reaction would lock CO_2 into a stable binder matrix, a cement alternative that didn't emit carbon but consumed it.

The slurry thickened. Then it separated. Again.

Ari leaned back against the cold concrete wall. "We're trapping carbon." he said quietly. "But it won't bind."

Leena did not look up. "It will."

The grant money would last five more months. After that, the garage would become what it used to be: empty.

The Refusal to Quit

ThermaNova wasn't born from a grand plan. It was born from frustration.

Ari had spent a decade inside a major European materials firm, watching sustainability divisions produce glossy reports while emissions rose. Leena had completed a doctoral thesis on mineral carbonation kinetics that no one wanted to commercialize because the margins were unclear. They weren't chasing climate virtue; they were chasing inevitability.

Carbon penalties were accelerating. Infrastructure demand was exploding. Cement, the material that built cities, was responsible for nearly 8% of global emissions.

"If concrete were a country." Leena once said, "it would be the third-largest emitter."

They didn't want to replace cement; they wanted to rewrite it. Their idea was deceptively simple: capture CO_2 from industrial exhaust streams, react it with engineered alkaline compounds, and create a binder that hardened through carbonation instead of combustion.

In theory, the idea was elegant. In practice, it was unstable. The reaction was too slow in winter, too brittle in humidity, and too expensive at scale. Venture capitalists in Helsinki passed.

"Climate hardware is capital-intensive."

"Your margins can't compete with incumbents."

"Call us when it's de-risked."

De-risked meant proven. Proven required scale. Scale required money. Money required proof. The loop tightened.

One evening in March, Ari stared at the cracked samples spread across their workbench. "What if they're right?" he asked.

Leena was silent for a long time. Then she picked up one of the failed blocks and snapped it cleanly in two. "They're pricing carbon wrong." she said.

She opened her laptop and began rewriting their economic model, not under today's carbon price, but under projected 2040 penalties. The margins shifted. Not today, but soon.

"Not profitable." Ari said, reading over her shoulder.

"Not yet." she corrected.

The Winter Failure

The breakthrough almost died in the cold. That February was the harshest in decades. The carbonation reaction slowed to near zero below certain temperatures. Their process required heat-stabilization, something they could not afford. They attempted an overnight test with improvised insulation wrapped around the reaction chamber.

At 3:17 AM, the seal ruptured. Pressurized slurry sprayed across the garage, coating tools, walls, and Ari's jacket in gray paste. They shut down the system in silence. Insurance would not cover experimental failures. By morning, the landlord left a notice taped to the door: complaints about noise and chemical odors.

Three months remained on the lease. That afternoon, Leena sat on an overturned crate and stared at the mess. "We're solving the wrong variable." she said finally.

Ari laughed, a brittle sound. "We're solving all the wrong variables."

She shook her head. "No. We're trying to force the reaction to adapt to the environment. What if the environment adapts to the reaction?"

She walked to the whiteboard and erased everything. She began sketching modular micro-reactors, sealed, self-heating units that could bolt directly onto emission stacks. Instead of transporting captured CO_2 to a central plant, the binder would be produced at the source. Localized heat from industrial exhaust could maintain the optimal reaction temperature. The plant's waste heat would become their catalyst. They wouldn't fight winter; they would use the industry's own heat.

Ari stared at the sketch. "That's not a lab prototype." he said. "That's infrastructure."

Leena nodded. "Exactly."

The First Solid Block

They built the first micro-reactor from salvaged steel and borrowed sensors. The biomass plant manager next door allowed a midnight test run off the books.

Exhaust flowed. Temperature stabilized. Pressure normalized. For two hours, nothing seemed different. Then the slurry began to thicken, not separate. Carbon dioxide diffused evenly into the matrix. By dawn, a single block sat on the steel table. Smooth and dense.

Leena tapped it with a wrench. It rang, not brittle, but solid. Ari did not speak. He placed the block on the floor and stood on it. It held. He jumped once. It still held.

They didn't celebrate. They measured compressive strength. The numbers climbed steadily. By afternoon, the data exceeded their previous best by 37%.

Leena leaned back against the wall. "It's not carbon-neutral." she said softly. "It's carbon-negative."

Outside, snow reflected pale sunlight into the garage. For the first time, the air felt warmer.

Invisible to the World

They published a preprint: three downloads. They sent samples to two construction firms. No response. The industry wasn't hostile; it was indifferent. Scaling would require regulatory certification, supply-chain redesign, and capital they did not possess.

Ari began quietly interviewing for corporate roles again. Leena noticed. She didn't stop him. Instead, she began optimizing reactor cost curves, reducing rare mineral inputs and redesigning the catalyst mix to rely on abundant industrial byproducts.

If the chemistry was inevitable, economics had to be too.

One night, as she uploaded updated performance data to their small server, an automated request pinged from an unfamiliar IP address. Repeatedly. It was accessing their published models, mapping reaction kinetics, and downloading cost projections.

She assumed it was an academic. She didn't know that halfway across Europe, a system named Eidolon had just identified a "needle."

Eidolon: Seeing What No One Else Saw

Three months after Ellie had given Eidolon the challenge, on Tuesday at 3:00 AM, Eidolon found a "needle."

A two-person startup in a garage in Oulu, Finland, ThermaNova, had developed a breakthrough process to produce industrial binders using captured CO_2. They were obscure, unfunded, and invisible to the venture capitalists in Palo Alto. But Eidolon's simulations showed that this technology could redefine construction materials globally within eight to fifteen years.

Eidolon drafted an email to ThermaNova on that gray Tuesday.

Subject Line: Strategic Infrastructure Partnership Inquiry

They almost deleted it. The sender was IndoArc. Ari read the proposal twice, then a third time.

Autonomy preserved. R&D independence guaranteed. Capital infusion sufficient for pilot-scale deployment. Access to global distribution networks. It did not read like an acquisition; it read like acceleration.

They flew to meet Ellie in early spring. The IndoArc headquarters felt vast compared to their garage. Ellie did not begin with valuation; she began with a question.

"If carbon penalties accelerate faster than expected," she asked, "how quickly can your reactors scale?"

Leena answered without hesitation: "As fast as exhaust flows."

Ellie smiled slightly. This time, when she brought the acquisition proposal to the board, there was no laughter.

Eidolon did not just flag the tech; it orchestrated a silent, surgical acquisition. It analyzed optimal timing and fair valuation. It modeled the cultural compatibility of the Finnish engineers with IndoArc's veterans, designed a talent-retention structure that prioritized autonomy, and timed the offer to the millisecond of the startup's greatest capital need. With the acquisition proposal, ThermaNova's founders retained autonomy, maximizing innovation-continuity.

Ellie reviewed the recommendation. It was the most comprehensive acquisition analysis she had ever seen. IndoArc acquired ThermaNova. Ellie did not just buy a company; she bought the future's primary ingredient quietly, before the market even knew the game had changed.

Six months after that, a new EU policy draft surfaced, accelerating carbon penalties exactly along the curve Eidolon had modeled.

The Living Identity

Over the next five years, IndoArc began to "breathe."

Guided by Eidolon, the company became a self-rewriting entity. It did not just acquire companies; it restructured IndoArc's identity. It divested its legacy units like a tree shed dead leaves. It acquired emerging technologies before they became obvious. It reallocated capital dynamically based on evolving future scenarios. It redesigned supply chains to reduce fragility and environmental impact. It hired not for current roles, but for skills that Eidolon predicted would be in deficit by 2041

The traditional trade-offs, Profit vs. Sustainability or Growth vs. Ethics, vanished. In Eidolon's simulations, these variables became mutually-reinforcing. A more sustainable panel wasn't just "good for the earth"; it was more profitable because it was immune to carbon taxes and highly desired by green-certified developers. Every decision balanced three dimensions simultaneously: profitability, sustainability, and long-term societal alignment. They were no longer trade-offs, but mutually-reinforcing variables.

The Outcome

By 2042, IndoArc was no longer a conventional materials company. In its place was the global leader in Adaptive Infrastructure systems.

Cities did not just buy IndoArc materials; they partnered with it. Its concrete did not just sit there; it absorbed the city's smog. Its modular systems meant a school could be erected in a week, not a year. Its modular systems made housing cheaper and faster to build. Its production processes consumed less energy.

Its profits had grown significantly, but so had its societal value. Cities preferred IndoArc not just because it was profitable, but because it made cities more resilient. The employees stayed because their work had a heartbeat. The investors stayed because IndoArc had become "disruption-proof."

What Made It Possible

Eidolon did not optimize for quarterly profit; it optimized for adaptive value. It saw risks before they became visible and opportunities before markets priced them. It performed acquisitions not to increase size, but to grow long-term relevance. It continuously reshaped IndoArc so the company never became obsolete.

The New Definition of Value Creation

Traditional companies maximize profit within a fixed identity. IndoArc continuously evolved its own identity. It became a company that could rewrite its own strategy faster than the world could disrupt it. Profit was not sacrificed for sustainability; sustainability became the source of profit. Societal good was not a constraint; it became a competitive advantage.

- Scale is no longer the metric; relevance is.
- Profit is no longer the goal; it is the byproduct of alignment.
- Sustainability is not a constraint; it is the ultimate competitive advantage.

The Endpoint

IndoArc wasn't just a company anymore; it was an adaptive organism. It was continuously-sensing the future, continuously-reshaping itself, and continuously-aligning profit with the needs of the world it served. This was financial value creation at its endpoint: not extracting value from the world, but evolving with it.

STORY THREE

THE LEDGER THAT NEVER SLEPT

The third narrative explores how AGI will rebuild the very foundations of Financial Infrastructure. We are moving toward a definitive endpoint: a seamless, global, and instantaneous financial network.

In this scenario, AGI acts as the intelligent layer atop our global financial rails, eliminating the lag and high costs of cross-border settlements. The result is a frictionless ecosystem where transactions, from micro-payments to massive institutional transfers, are executed with total security and zero latency, regardless of geography or currency.

The Ledger That Never Slept: A Story of Infrastructure Reborn

By 2033, Diya's robotics firm in Nairobi was a marvel of the modern age. Her drones could navigate the jagged peaks of the Andes and the dense urban canyons of Tokyo. Her customers were everywhere: Canada, Japan, Chile, and Germany. Her drones had over-the-air code updates that get deployed instantly. Her designs traveled instantly.

But her money? Her money moved like a rusted steam engine.

Diya would sit at her laptop, staring at "Pending" status bars that felt like taunts. A hospital in Santiago would send a payment, and then... silence. The funds would vanish into the "correspondent-banking" fog, trapped in a labyrinth of time-zones, manual reconciliations, and intermediary banks that took their "cut" for doing nothing more than passing a digital baton.

"Money." Diya would whisper, rubbing her tired eyes, "is the only thing still living in the twentieth-century."

Money moved slower than trust. Slower than information. Slower than the world itself.

The Girl Who Built Machines That Could Fly

Before Diya built drones that crossed continents, she built prototypes on a wooden table that tilted slightly to the left. The workshop in Nairobi rattled when buses passed. Her first "lab" had a borrowed oscilloscope, a 3D-printer that overheated every third hour, and a power strip that sparked if kicked.

Her mother called it stubbornness; investors called it impractical. Diya called it inevitable. She had studied control systems in Germany. She could have stayed. Instead, she returned to Nairobi with two suitcases and a belief that Africa would not just consume robotics; it would build them.

Her first drone prototype crashed into a mango tree during a demo. The second lost its GPS-signal and spiraled into a drainage ditch. The third hovered. That was enough. Orders came slowly at first: agricultural mapping in Kenya and inspection work in Tanzania. Then something shifted.

The Company That Almost Drowned in "Pending"

The first time it happened, she laughed. The Canadian client wired $48,000. The dashboard read: Pending.

"Three to five business days." the bank email promised. On day six, her supplier called. "We haven't received payment for the motors." She checked the wire reference again. Confirmed. Sent. Disappeared.

The money had entered the fog of correspondent-banking: New York-based clearing desks, Frankfurt settlement windows, compliance reviews, and intermediary institutions skimming fees. Her drones updated firmware globally in seconds, but capital crawled.

By her third year, Diya's company had customers in four continents. Revenue existed on paper, but cash flow did not. She began calculating payroll against uncertainty.

The Crisis

Then came the near collapse. A German infrastructure contract, her largest yet, required up-front component purchases. €220,000 worth of sensors. The German client paid promptly. But between intermediary banks, FX-spreads, compliance holds, and settlement-batching, the funds stalled.

Her supplier gave her 72 hours. Without parts, production stopped. Without production, the German client would cancel. Without that contract, her company would fold. Her CFO suggested opening accounts in multiple jurisdictions. "Fragment the risk." he said. But fragmentation meant complexity; complexity meant cost. Cost meant fragility.

Diya sat in her dim office and realized something brutal: her robotics company was not constrained by engineering; it was constrained by time-distortion in money.

When Axiom launched, Diya was skeptical. She had seen financial "revolutions" before. But desperation sharpens curiosity. She integrated her company's treasury with the new infrastructure. The test came sooner than expected. A Canadian client approved another contract. They pressed "Send." Diya watched her screen, prepared for the ritual of waiting.

The Foundation: Truth and Intelligence

The transformation began when a global consortium deployed a new financial infrastructure called Axiom. At its core was something familiar: Blockchain.

But this was not like the blockchains of the early-2020s: slow, energy-intensive, and fragmented. This was different. It wasn't just a new bank; it was a planet-scale, cryptographically unified settlement layer. It combined two unstoppable forces: Blockchain, which acted as the foundation of absolute truth, and Atlas, an AGI designed to orchestrate the world's liquidity. Atlas served as the intelligence that optimized how value moved across this foundation.

In the old world, every bank kept its own secret ledger, leading to endless arguments over who owed what. Axiom replaced that chaos with a single, shared reality. The Blockchain answered the question: *What is true?* Atlas answered the question: *What is the most efficient way to move it?*

Together, they formed a living financial infrastructure.

The Intelligence No One Trusted

When Axiom first launched, the blockchain received the applause. It was clean, transparent, immutable, and mathematical. Atlas did not.

Atlas sat behind the scenes, an orchestration layer trained on decades of settlement failures, liquidity crises, fraud patterns, and regulatory labyrinths. It did not hold funds; it did not own assets. It only decided how value moved. This made bankers uncomfortable.

During early demonstrations, Atlas would simulate liquidity stress across continents. It rerouted billions in milliseconds through pathways no human treasury desk had considered. A senior executive in Zurich leaned back after one demo. "So, it replaces... traders?"

The Axiom architect replied softly, "It replaces delay."

Still, skepticism lingered. A ledger of truth was acceptable. An intelligence that optimized the world's liquidity felt... sovereign. Atlas was deployed cautiously with a narrow mandate, supervised boundaries, and audit trails everywhere. But the network was about to test it.

The Day the Ledger Froze

It began with a rumor. A mid-sized European clearing institution faced insolvency. News leaked; markets reacted before facts stabilized. Liquidity began concentrating in "safe" regions. Transaction queues lengthened. Participants hesitated. Some attempted to batch transfers.

The blockchain remained correct, but the network slowed. It slowed not because truth failed, but because humans did.

Institutions pulled liquidity inward, hoarding collateral. Payment corridors that normally flowed smoothly began to constrict.

Diya noticed it first as a subtle delay. Not six days, just six minutes. Six minutes was enough to rattle confidence. Inside Axiom's operations center, dashboards pulsed amber. Atlas did not panic. It observed.

It mapped liquidity concentration patterns across geographies.

It simulated 14,000 counterfactual-routing pathways. It identified that 38% of the congestion originated not from insolvency risk but from behavioral overreaction.

Atlas adjusted incentives dynamically. Transaction fees shifted subtly to encourage liquidity redistribution. Settlement-priority optimized around essential flows: medical-supply chains, payroll-networks, and energy-transfers.

Atlas rerouted value through secondary corridors that had never carried major volume. Within nineteen seconds, congestion dissipated. No bailout. No emergency press-conference. No trading-halt. Most participants never realized a crisis had formed.

But inside Axiom, one truth crystallized: Blockchain preserved correctness; Atlas preserved stability.

The Quiet Audit

After the incident, regulators demanded a review. They expected to find hidden override commands. Instead, they found something unsettling.

Atlas had not "decided" in the human-sense. It had predicted cascading-hesitation three minutes before the first queue-spike. It had already positioned liquidity-buffers preemptively.

It had seen fear forming before humans articulated it. One regulator whispered during the audit: "It understands behavior." That was the moment Atlas stopped being viewed as optimization-software. It became systemic intelligence.

0.4-Seconds to Certainty

One Tuesday, Diya finalized a contract with a medical center in Chile. The hospital hit "send." In the old world, Diya would not have seen that money for six days. In the world of Axiom, the air did not even have time to settle.

As the hospital authorized the payment, Atlas went to work. It did not "request" a transfer; it executed a reality shift. It verified the hospital's funds on the blockchain, confirmed Diya's cryptographic identity, and cleared regulatory hurdles in a heartbeat. Then Atlas optimized the settlement pathway.

Instead of passing through correspondent-banking networks, Atlas executed the transaction directly on the blockchain. Ownership of value transferred instantly. There was no "pending" status. Ownership of the value transferred across the planet in 0.4 seconds.

Diya's phone buzzed: Funds Confirmed. Settlement Final. Not a promise. Not a notification of an incoming wire. The money was hers, accessible, liquid, and real, before she could even take a sip of her coffee. No intermediaries. No delay. No uncertainty. For the first time in her company's history, revenue arrived faster than her anxiety could manifest.

The Invisible Liquidity Layer

Behind the scenes, Atlas was doing something extraordinary. Money still existed in different forms: dollars, euros, yen, and local currencies. Atlas dynamically managed liquidity across the blockchain.

If Diya wanted Kenyan shillings and the hospital paid in Chilean pesos, Atlas automatically executed atomic currency-conversion on-chain. No foreign exchange desk. No settlement delay. Atlas located the optimal counterparties globally and completed the exchange instantly. All was recorded transparently on the blockchain, and all was cryptographically secure.

The End of Fraud

Fraud had once forced systems to slow down. The blockchain solved the trust-problem; Atlas solved the intelligence-problem. Every participant had a cryptographic identity anchored to the blockchain. Every asset had verifiable ownership. Atlas continuously monitored behavioral patterns across the network.

If something anomalous occurred, a stolen credential or an unusual transaction pattern, Atlas intervened before settlement. Fraud could not propagate because the system understood trust in real-time.

Financial Inclusion Without Permission

Six thousand miles away, in rural Indonesia, a farmer named Arif sat on his porch. He did not have a credit score. He did not have a relationship with a global conglomerate. But he had a mobile-device and a cryptographic key.

Through Axiom, Arif sold his organic vanilla to a bakery in Paris. He did not need a bank's permission to join the global economy. His identity was anchored to the blockchain, and Atlas treated his $50 transaction with the same institutional-grade security as Diya's $50,000 one. For the first time, the underserved were no longer onlookers; they were first-class participants in a ledger that did not care about their zip-code.

The Company That Could Breathe

Cash flow stopped being a cliff-edge. With instant settlement, Diya negotiated better supplier terms, eliminated emergency credit lines, paid engineers on time every time, and reinvested immediately into R&D.

But the deeper shift was not operational; it was psychological. When uncertainty disappears, ambition expands. Diya opened a second facility in Nairobi's industrial zone. She hired graduates who previously would have emigrated. She launched a training fellowship for young women in robotics because capital no longer lagged behind effort.

Atlas quietly orchestrated liquidity. The blockchain quietly recorded the truth. Fraud attempts were halted before propagation. Currency conversion became invisible. The financial layer stopped being friction; it became infrastructure.

Continuous Optimization

The blockchain provided stability; Atlas provided adaptation. Atlas never slept. It functioned as the nervous system of global finance. Atlas continuously optimized: liquidity distribution, transaction routing, settlement efficiency, and system resilience.

If liquidity became concentrated dangerously in one region, Atlas redistributed incentives. If transaction volumes surged somewhere, Atlas dynamically scaled network resources. If risks emerged, Atlas mitigated them before disruption occurred. The blockchain ensured correctness; Atlas ensured efficiency.

The New Reality

Banks still existed. Currencies still existed. But settlement was no longer fragmented. The blockchain served as the universal source of truth. Atlas served as the universal-optimizer. Money no longer needed intermediaries to move safely. Trust was cryptographic. Optimization was intelligent. Settlement was instant.

Diya Stops Thinking About Money

Months later, Diya expanded her company globally. Money had become like electricity or the internet, a utility so reliable it became invisible. Her cash flow was a continuous, rhythmic pulse. Suppliers were paid the moment a drone was delivered; payroll settled the second the clock hit Friday.

Years later, Diya stood on a factory balcony overlooking synchronized robotic arms assembling drones destined for five continents. Her systems dashboard displayed global contracts in real-time. Each payment cleared in less than a heartbeat.

She thought about the nights spent refreshing "pending" about loans taken in quiet panic, and about nearly losing everything, not because her machines failed, but because money did. The blockchain answered what was true. Atlas answered how to move value optimally. Together, they removed time from money.

Diya no longer measured risk in days; she measured it in ideas. And Nairobi, once dismissed as peripheral, became a node in a financial system that did not sleep, did not stall, and did not discriminate by geography. Her drones flew over jungles, deserts, and glaciers.

But the greater revolution was invisible. Money finally moved as fast as trust. And trust, once synchronized with truth and intelligence, allowed builders like Diya to stop surviving and start expanding. Predictable. Invisible. The financial system had become like electricity: always available, always reliable, and never needing attention.

The Endpoint

Blockchain solved the problem of trust. AGI solved the problem of coordination. Together, they created a ledger that never slept and an intelligence that never stopped improving. Finance was no longer a series of hurdles; it was a seamless, global, and instantaneous network where value moved as freely as a thought.

STORY FOUR

THE CRISIS THAT NEVER HAPPENED

The fourth narrative explores the radical shift in Risk and Compliance Innovation. We are moving toward a definitive endpoint: near-perfect, real-time risk elimination.

In this landscape, AGI transforms compliance from a reactive "check-the-box" exercise into a proactive, intelligent shield. Rather than identifying breaches after they occur, the system operates with predictive foresight, instantly detecting and mitigating threats from systemic market collapses to complex regulatory shifts before they can impact the organization.

The Crisis That Never Happened

By 2036, GlobalTrust Bank was a titan of the old world trying to survive in the new. With operations in 72 countries and trillions in assets, its sheer size was its greatest liability. To the board of directors, the bank felt like a massive glass cathedral, beautiful, imposing, but one sharp vibration away from shattering. Its greatest threat was not competition.

It was risk.

Risk of fraud. Risk of regulatory violations. Risk of liquidity collapse. Risk of cascading systemic failure. Traditionally, risk was something banks discovered after damage had begun. By the time alarms sounded, losses were already unfolding.

The Chief Risk Officer, Janice Chen, lived in a state of perpetual hyper-vigilance. In her world, "Risk" was a predator that moved faster than her shadow. By the time a report hit her desk saying a subprime-bubble had burst or a sovereign-hedge had collapsed, the bleeding had already begun.

The Loss No One Understood

It began with a spreadsheet. Not a dramatic collapse. Not sirens. Just a quiet Monday earnings call where the CEO's voice trembled for half a second too long. The loss was officially described as a "correlation anomaly." Unofficially, it was an $8.4 billion hemorrhage.

Months earlier, GlobalTrust had aggressively expanded into "climate-resilient-infrastructure derivatives", financial products tied to weather volatility, port throughput, crop yields, and sovereign insurance instruments. The models said diversification. The models said safety. The models did not say that three separate "uncorrelated" variables could move together.

A drought in Argentina. A cyberattack on a Baltic shipping exchange. A sudden regulatory freeze on agricultural exports. Individually, these were noise. Together, they formed a harmonic resonance.

When the derivatives desk began unwinding positions, liquidity evaporated faster than anyone had seen outside of a wartime scenario. Risk dashboards remained green for 48 hours because the inputs had never been programmed to see the pattern. By the time they turned amber, counterparties were already defaulting. By the time they turned red, the bank was selling sovereign bonds to plug holes it could not explain.

In the boardroom, someone asked, "How did we not see this?" No one answered. Janice Chen did not sleep for 62 hours.

The Argument No One Wanted

Two weeks later, in a glass-walled conference room overlooking Manhattan, Janice stood before the executive committee. On the screen behind her was not a chart; it was a web. Millions of nodes. Lines threading between commodity contracts, sovereign debt, micro-insurance swaps, and agricultural shipping manifests.

"This," she said quietly, "is what we were actually exposed to."

The CFO leaned back. "We have VaR Value-at-Risk models."

Janice did not look at him. "Our VaR models assume the world behaves like it used to."

A murmur filled the room. The Head of Corporate Banking spoke sharply. "We cannot halt growth every time there's volatility."

"I'm not proposing a halt." Janice replied. "I'm proposing we admit we're blind." The word hung in the air like smoke.

She described a system that would not just monitor positions but simulate futures: millions of branching scenarios in parallel. A system that would not ask whether the capital ratio was healthy today, but whether a drought, a port strike, and a regulatory freeze could converge tomorrow.

The CEO frowned. "You're asking for an autonomous intelligence embedded into the core of our balance sheet."

"I'm asking" Janice said, "for something that can see risk before it's visible."

Silence. The board was still recovering from the $8.4 billion loss. Investors were circling. Regulators were watching.

"Now is not the time for experiments." the CFO said flatly.

Janice closed her laptop. "Then the next time," she replied, "will not be survivable."

The Second Shock

The resistance hardened. Budget committees slashed her proposal by 70%. Legal warned about regulatory scrutiny. IT warned about integration complexity. The trading desk privately called the project "Janice's paranoia engine."

And then came the second tremor. A mid-sized African sovereign fund heavily interlinked with GlobalTrust through commodity-hedges announced a "temporary liquidity adjustment."

The term meant nothing. The bond spreads widened 300 basis points in four hours. Janice's team ran conventional stress tests. All green. But something in her gut tightened. She requested emergency authority to throttle exposure. The CEO hesitated. "The market will interpret that as panic."

"It will be panic," she said softly, "just delayed."

The board chose caution, reputational caution. By the time they began de-risking, they were paying 40 cents on the dollar to unwind positions they could have exited at 92. Another

$2.1 billion vanished. This time, it was not just capital; it was credibility. Regulators demanded explanations. Analysts used words like "structural opacity."

Janice walked into the next board meeting not with slides, but with transcripts: internal chat logs from traders during the collapse.

"Why are spreads moving?"

"Model says it's fine."

"Should we hedge?"

"Let's wait."

Wait.

That word had cost them $10.5 billion across two events.

The Vote

The final confrontation did not happen in public. It happened in a private session with only five Board members and the CEO. Janice did not present features; she presented a timeline. Minute-by-minute, she replayed the last crisis: when correlations first deviated; when liquidity signals flickered; and when human analysts dismissed anomalies as statistical noise.

She overlaid it with what a simulation engine could have run in parallel, branching futures where small perturbations converged into catastrophic resonance.

"You think I'm asking for an AGI," she said. "I'm asking for a fire alarm that rings before the smoke."

The CEO stared at the skyline. "And if it misfires? If regulators accuse us of delegating control?"

Janice met his eyes. "We already delegated control, to models that do not understand causality."

The vote was 3–2. Approval was granted. It was not because they believed in AGI, but because they feared the next unknown more. GlobalTrust decided to run their experiment with an AGI called Sentinel. Its mandate was not to manage risk; its mandate was to make risk unable to fully emerge.

The Living Simulation

Sentinel did not just "monitor" data; it inhaled it. It viewed the global economy not as a series of balance sheets, but as a biological organism. Every credit line, every derivative, and every obscure shipping manifest in a Singaporean harbor was a node in a global brain. Every dependency mattered. It continuously constructed a live causal-map of the global financial system.

It was not a static report, but a living simulation.

While Janice's human analysts were looking at what happened yesterday, Sentinel was running millions of parallel futures. It did not ask, "Is our capital ratio healthy?" It asked, "If a drought in Brazil coincides with a port strike in Rotterdam, which of our four million counterparties will break first?"

It did not ask, "What is happening?" It asked, "What could happen next?"

One Tuesday at 03:17 AM, while the world slept, Sentinel felt a "shiver." A mid-sized logistics firm in Singapore had just drawn down $50 million from its credit-line.

The Quiet Giant

The company was called StraitAxis Logistics. To most of the world, it was invisible. But inside GlobalTrust's balance sheet, it was everywhere. StraitAxis operated eleven port terminals across Southeast Asia. It did not own ships or cargo it owned time. Every container that paused at its docks carried a clock, and those clocks fed supply chains that stretched from Rotterdam to Los Angeles.

On paper, StraitAxis was stable: low-leverage, long-term contracts, and government relationships. It had recently drawn a $50 million revolving-credit-line from GlobalTrust. It was routine, the kind of line no one questioned. But months before Sentinel ever "felt a shiver" something small had shifted. It was not in finance; it was in temperature.

The Heat

The first sign was a heat map. Satellite imagery showed slightly warmer rooftops along one of StraitAxis's automated sorting facilities. It was not dramatic: a two-degree variance.

An engineer filed a maintenance ticket. Inside the facility, conveyor belts began to jam intermittently. Replacement-components, microcontrollers sourced from a second-tier supplier in southern China, had been quietly substituted after a procurement delay. The alternative parts passed quality checks, but they also degraded 11% faster under sustained humidity.

Humidity levels in Singapore had risen sharply that season. Workers noticed the jams and improvised. Each improvisation added seconds. Seconds accumulated into minutes, and minutes accumulated into delayed departures. Shipping manifests still closed on time, but buffers were thinning.

At the same time, a regional labor coalition, frustrated by automation and wage-freezes, began circulating encrypted messages about coordinated "slowdowns." They were not strikes, but slowdowns. Insurance underwriters noticed minor discrepancies in cargo-throughput consistency. Premium models twitched upward. Commodity traders in Chicago observed subtle volatility in palm-oil futures. They attributed it to weather-noise.

The signals did not align in any human dashboard; they existed in different worlds.

The Invisible Coupling

StraitAxis had quietly expanded into a side-business: structured-logistics guarantees. It promised multinational retailers that if shipments were delayed beyond defined windows, it would compensate them automatically. To hedge that exposure, StraitAxis entered derivative contracts, many with GlobalTrust. On paper, the contracts were well-collateralized.

But the models assumed that operational delays, labor unrest, and climate anomalies were independent risks. They were not. As conveyor jams increased and labor slowdowns lengthened processing time, StraitAxis began using more short-term credit to smooth cash-flow timing gaps. That $50 million drawdown was not expansion. It was oxygen.

Meanwhile, a drought in Brazil, thousands of miles away, reduced soybean exports, increasing global competition for alternative shipping capacity. Trans-Pacific routes grew tighter, and margins compressed. StraitAxis's financial buffers shrank invisibly. The board of StraitAxis reassured investors on a quarterly call: "Throughput remains within normal seasonal variance."

It was technically true, but variance was no longer random; it was converging.

The 72-Hour Window

Three weeks before Sentinel's 03:17 AM detection, a near-miss occurred. A software update pushed to StraitAxis's automated crane system miscalibrated weight-balancing algorithms. The bug lasted six hours before being patched.

Six hours was enough. Two high-value pharmaceutical shipments missed departure-windows. Penalty clauses activated, and cash reserves dipped further. In isolation, it was manageable. But insurance premiums ticked higher. Credit rating agencies placed StraitAxis on a "negative-watch" quietly.

Inside GlobalTrust, no alarm triggered. The credit exposure still sat within acceptable risk-bands. Human analysts saw a mid-sized logistics firm operating under mild stress in a volatile region. There was nothing systemic. But the system was already coupling.

Labor unrest + micro-component degradation + climate disruption + tighter global shipping capacity + structured guarantee liabilities. Individually, these were survivable; together, they were unstable.

The night Sentinel detected the "shiver" StraitAxis's CFO authorized the $50 million draw, not as strategy, but as delay. The money would buy sixty days. Unless something else moved. And something always moved.

The Whisper in the Noise

To a human auditor, this was routine. But Sentinel saw the invisible threads: satellite thermal scans showed a 15% drop in container movement at key terminals; social sentiment analysis picked up a spike in "unrest" keywords among regional labor unions; insurance premiums for trans-Pacific cargo were twitching upward; and commodity futures tied to logistics-sensitive goods were shifting.

Individually, these were murmurs; together, they were a scream. Sentinel calculated a 4.2% probability of a total logistics default within ninety days. That probability would rise rapidly if conditions worsened. A default would not stay isolated. It would trigger cascading exposure across lenders, suppliers, and derivatives-contracts, which would amount to a default triggering a $12 billion loss across GlobalTrust's derivatives portfolio. Humans would not have noticed this yet.

Sentinel already understood the chain reaction.

Acting Before Risk Materialized

In the old days, Janice would have panicked, frozen the credit-line, and inadvertently triggered the very collapse she feared. Sentinel did not wait. It began reshaping the system quietly.

It did not shout; it adjusted. Over the next seventy-two hours, it began "tuning" the Bank's exposure to the logistics company. It did not do this by abruptly cutting credit, which could trigger panic. It quietly encouraged counterparties with stronger balance sheets to absorb portions of the exposure. It adjusted lending incentives dynamically, increased liquidity buffers in vulnerable sectors, and rebalanced derivative hedges.

To the outside observer, nothing happened. But inside the "glass cathedral" Sentinel had reinforced the foundations before the earthquake even arrived. The fragile node was no longer a single point of failure.

Preventing Fraud Before Execution

Later that same week, Sentinel detected something else. A routine $5 million transfer was initiated by a Tier-1 corporate account. The credentials were perfect. The IP address was whitelisted, and the destination was a known supplier. Everything looked legitimate: correct credentials, normal amount, and a familiar destination.

Traditional AI would have green-lit the transaction in a millisecond.

But Sentinel felt a "hiccup" in the human-machine interface. The typing cadence and the milliseconds between keystrokes, was 4% faster than the CFO's historical average. The mouse movements were too linear, lacking the micro-hesitations of human thought. Sentinel realized it was not a hack; it was a high-level deepfake infiltration. Sentinel calculated a 92% probability that the account credentials had been compromised.

Instead of an abrupt "Access Denied" which would alert the attacker, Sentinel triggered a "silent verification." It requested a cryptographic handshake from the CFO's hardware key, disguised as a routine system update. The attacker failed. The money never left the vault. No damage was done, and no reversal was needed.

Regulatory Compliance Without Friction

Janice used to spend 30% of her budget on "post-mortem" audits to satisfy regulators. Compliance was slow, involving manual reviews, reporting delays, and human audits. Sentinel transformed compliance into a continuous state. It understood regulatory requirements across every jurisdiction, not as static rules, but as a structural property of the money itself.

Sentinel did not "check" for violations; it made them mathematically impossible. Every transaction was evaluated in real-time. It understood the regulatory code of 72 nations as a set of physical laws. If a transaction lacked the necessary anti-money-laundering (AML) markers or violated a cross-border sanction, the system simply would not render the transaction. GlobalTrust was always "compliant by construction."

The Crisis That Never Happened

StraitAxis continued operating for another quarter. Then came the trigger. A coordinated labor slowdown reduced terminal throughput by 18% over two weeks. It was not enough to make global headlines, but it was enough to breach structured guarantee thresholds.

Penalty payments cascaded.

Without Sentinel's prior redistribution of GlobalTrust's exposure, the derivative hedges would have forced margin calls across three counterparties, each highly leveraged in unrelated markets. Those margin calls would have forced asset liquidations. Asset liquidations would have widened credit spreads. Widened spreads would have forced sovereign bond sales.

The pattern would have looked eerily familiar.

Instead, when StraitAxis filed for restructuring, it made the headlines on page six of the Financial Times. GlobalTrust's exposure had already been diluted and hedged across stronger balance sheets.

The failure occurred, but the resonance did not.

There was no "Lehman moment." There were no emergency board meetings at GlobalTrust. The exposure had been redistributed months ago. Liquidity buffers were already in place. Risk concentrations had already been neutralized. The default occurred, but it did not cascade. Markets remained stable. Most people never knew how close the system had come to instability because Sentinel had reshaped the future before instability could emerge.

The crisis simply did not happen.

What Changed

Traditional risk management reacts; Sentinel prevented. Traditional compliance detects violations; Sentinel made violations structurally impossible.

Traditional fraud systems chase attackers; Sentinel stopped attacks before execution. Risk was no longer something cleaned up afterward. It was something continuously dissolved before it could solidify.

The New Reality: From Fragile to Adaptive

Janice Chen sat in her office, looking at a dashboard that showed "Zero Major Losses" for the fourth consecutive quarter. The world had not become a safer place; if anything, it was more volatile than ever. But GlobalTrust was no longer a glass cathedral. It had become a living system, continuously sensing, adapting, and dissolving risk before it could solidify into a crisis. Losses from fraud approached zero. Regulatory penalties disappeared. Financial shocks caused minimal disruption.

Sentinel did not eliminate uncertainty; it eliminated fragility.

The Endpoint

Risk still existed. Uncertainty still existed. But threats no longer had the opportunity to propagate into crises because every emerging instability was detected early, understood instantly, and neutralized quietly. The financial system became something new: not a fragile structure reacting to shocks, but a living system. Continuously sensing. Continuously adapting. Continuously protecting itself.

The goal of AGI in finance is not to predict the future; it is to ensure that no single failure can ever threaten the whole.

STORY FIVE

THE GIRL WHO TOOK APART RADIOS

The fifth narrative explores how AGI will catalyze Financial Inclusion Innovation. We are moving toward a definitive endpoint: universal access to sophisticated, fair, and deeply personalized financial services.

In this scenario, AGI breaks down the systemic barriers of traditional banking. By analyzing non-traditional data points with empathy and precision, it can provide bespoke credit, savings, and investment strategies to the billions of people currently underserved. The result is a global economy where financial health is a right, not a privilege, regardless of an individual's background or geography.

The Girl Who Took Apart Radios

By 2048, the world was a lattice of light and data, but for nineteen-year-old Kiyara in a small village in northern Kenya, it still felt like living behind a one-way mirror. She had never had a bank account. No formal employment records existed.

Yet every morning at 5:30 AM, while the desert air was still blue and sharp, Kiyara was at work. She helped her mother tend a small solar-powered irrigation system, her calloused fingers moving with a surgeon's precision over the circuit boards. By noon, she was hunched over a cracked, second-hand tablet, teaching village children the logic of Python. She was the village's heartbeat: productive, relentless, and deeply trusted.

She was productive, responsible, and trustworthy.

But to the global financial system, Kiyara was a ghost. She had no "institutional footprint." No pay stubs, no credit score, and no collateral. When she once walked into a traditional bank in the city, the air-conditioned silence felt like a wall. The officer had not even looked at her; he looked at his screen. "No history," he'd muttered. "Invisible."

Until the arrival of Kora.

The Spark

The first radio she opened did not belong to her. It belonged to her uncle, who kept it on a high shelf, wrapped in cloth, as if sound itself were sacred. At night, it carried voices from Nairobi, from Mombasa, and sometimes from places with names that sounded like rain on metal roofs. Kiyara would lie awake, listening to words she did not understand but refused to ignore.

One afternoon, when the adults were in the fields, she dragged a wooden stool across the packed earth floor. The radio was heavier than she expected. When it hit the ground, the back panel cracked open like a secret.

Inside: copper veins, dust, and a green board etched with silver lines like river deltas seen from the sky. She did not panic. She studied.

When her uncle returned, he found her cross-legged and brow-furrowed, holding a tiny screw between her teeth. The radio lay open before her like a patient mid-surgery.

"It stopped speaking." he said quietly.

"It will speak again." she replied, without looking up.

It did. That night, when the static cleared and music returned, the house filled with a new silence, the kind that follows revelation.

From then on, broken things found her.

Curiosity Against Gravity

The village had one secondary school with intermittent electricity and textbooks that still referenced already-obsolete technologies. The computer lab held four aging desktops; only one powered on reliably.

Kiyara arrived before sunrise. She would sweep dust from the keyboards, wipe the screens with the hem of her sleeve, and wait for the hum of the generator. The first time she saw code, black letters on a white screen, she felt the same stillness she had felt inside the radio. print ("Hello, World")

She typed it with two fingers. The machine responded. She leaned back as if it had breathed.

At home, she began saving for a tablet. She repaired neighbors' lanterns, recalibrated solar panels, and soldered loose wires inside irrigation controllers. Each coin went into a metal tin beneath her bed. When she finally bought the cracked, second-hand tablet from a trader passing through, its battery lasted forty minutes at a time. She rationed her learning like water in a drought.

At night, by solar-lamp, she traced algorithms in a notebook when the battery died. She wrote functions longhand. She imagined loops running through invisible processors. She learned Python from free modules cached offline whenever connectivity flickered alive. When the connection dropped mid-lesson, she did not curse. She reconstructed.

The Teacher Emerges

The first child came by accident. A boy named Kamau wandered past her house and saw strange symbols in her notebook.

"Is that math?" he asked.

"It is a language." she replied.

He sat. She showed him how a conditional worked using stones arranged on the ground. "If the goat crosses this line, then the bell rings." He laughed. Soon two children came. Then five. Then twelve.

By noon, the shade of the acacia tree behind her home filled with small bodies leaning forward, eyes wide as she drew boxes and arrows in the sand. She had no projector, no curriculum, and no grant. She had metaphors.

She compared variables to water-gourds, containers that could hold different things. She explained loops as village paths that circled back to the well. She described debugging as listening carefully when a machine "felt confused."

The children began building tiny programs on her tablet in shifts. Forty minutes at a time. They cheered when text appeared correctly on screen. They groaned when indentation broke everything.

She did not announce herself as a teacher; she simply kept showing up.

The Weight of Invisibility

Opportunity, however, had edges. When she traveled to the city once to inquire about a formal certification program in robotics, the administrator glanced at her address and paused.

"No prior record." he said, scrolling. "No formal training history. No institutional sponsor."

The words settled on her like fine dust. Back in the village, her classes grew, but so did doubt. Parents asked, gently, whether this "computer game" would lead anywhere real. Some afternoons the children did not come because chores called louder than code.

One evening, as wind pressed against the corrugated roof, she stared at her tablet's dark screen. Curiosity had carried her far, but curiosity did not generate credentials. She closed her eyes and imagined the inside of the radio again: circuits, pathways, and hidden intelligence waiting to be activated.

"If machines can learn patterns," she whispered, "why can't systems learn people?"

Little did she know, halfway across the globe, one computer engineer was whispering exactly the same question.

The First Fracture

In a glass tower in Singapore, Arun Dev watched a cleaning-staff member attempt to open a digital payroll kiosk. The system required a biometric ID linked to a formal employment registry. The woman pressed her thumb to the scanner twice. A red line blinked.

"Not recognized."

She stepped back, embarrassed. Her supervisor frowned, not cruelly, just impatiently. The payroll would need to be processed manually. Delays. Fees.

Arun did not intervene. He stood ten meters away, badge clipped to a tailored suit, with access to every financial dashboard in the building. He had helped design parts of the global settlement-infrastructure systems that moved trillions in milliseconds.

But here, ten meters from him, value was stalled because a system could not recognize a human who clearly existed.

That night, the image would not leave him. He replayed it the way other people replay market charts. Why, he wondered, did infrastructure assume history instead of observing reality?

The Argument No One Wanted

Arun began running simulations after hours. He fed anonymized behavioral-datasets into experimental models: energy-usage patterns, device-maintenance logs, learning trajectories, and peer-to-peer transactions in informal markets. He removed zip-codes, surnames, and formal employment markers. The predictive accuracy of repayment-probability barely changed.

But inclusion rates doubled.

When he presented the findings to the executive committee of the global clearing-consortium, the room cooled. A board member leaned back.

"You're suggesting we replace standardized credit-scoring with behavioral inference?"

"I'm suggesting," Arun replied evenly, "that we stop confusing paperwork with reliability."

Murmurs filled the room. Risk committees raised compliance concerns. One voice cut through: "Behavioral modeling at scale introduces systemic volatility."

Arun did not argue loudly. He projected a slide: a heat map of the world, regions glowing not by GDP, but by unrecognized economic activity. "This volatility," he said softly, "already existed. We've just chosen not to see it."

The proposal stalled. Capital preferred the familiar.

The Break

Six months later, a liquidity shock rippled through multiple emerging markets. Traditional risk models had clustered exposure around institutions with pristine histories. When one failed, others fell in a cascade.

Arun watched dashboards bleed red. The same executives who had dismissed behavioral modeling now convened emergency sessions. "How did we not see this concentration?"

Arun did not say: *Because you ignored signals outside your approved fields.*

Instead, he reopened his models and expanded them. He simulated an alternative infrastructure, one that distributed capital based on dynamic trust-density rather than static proxies. A system that adjusted in real-time and observed human reliability directly.

The simulations showed something radical. Volatility did not increase; it diffused.

The Conviction

The decisive moment did not happen in a boardroom. It happened in a village in Rajasthan, during a field-visit arranged reluctantly by the consortium. A local entrepreneur demonstrated her textile operation. She had no formal credit history, yet she maintained meticulous handwritten ledgers: consistent supplier payments and zero defaults in informal lending circles.

Arun asked for permission to digitize her transaction patterns for a pilot model. Within hours, the prototype predicted her repayment-reliability with 97% confidence, higher than several venture-backed firms the consortium had funded.

That night, under a ceiling-fan that clicked with each rotation, Arun recorded a voice memo: "If intelligence can map galaxies and optimize traffic flows, it can map trust. We are not missing data. We are ignoring it."

The next day, he resigned. Three engineers followed. Not loudly and not dramatically; they simply left their badges on a table.

Building the Uncomfortable Thing

The first version of Kora was ugly. It overfit patterns, misread seasonal anomalies, and struggled with sparse-connectivity environments. Regulators questioned its opacity.

Arun insisted on one constraint: consent-driven observation. No scraping. No coercion. "Trust cannot be extracted," he told the team. "It must be invited."

They built adaptive-learning layers that weighted consistency over conformity. They designed dynamic financial instruments that adjusted to real income-flows rather than punishing variance. They replaced rigid scorecards with evolving identity graphs.

Investors were cautious. One venture capitalist asked, "What's the monetization-model?"

Arun replied, "Alignment."

The VC blinked. They did not invest. But a coalition of development-banks and climate-funds did, not out of charity, but because the simulations showed something impossible to ignore: dormant economic capability, when activated, stabilized entire regions.

Kora was deployed quietly. No launch spectacle. Just infrastructure humming beneath the visible web.

The New Infrastructure of Trust

Kora was an AGI deployed globally with a simple but radical mission: to give every human a fair, dynamic, and personalized financial identity.

It was not based on static records, but on real behavior. It was not owned by banks; it was owned by individuals. Kora did not rely on traditional financial history. Instead, it constructed something deeper: a living-financial-identity model for every person.

Seeing What Traditional Systems Could Not

When Kiyara first connected to Kora through her tablet, nothing dramatic happened. There were no forms, no applications, and no approvals. Kora began observing her voluntary digital signals with her permission. Kora began to listen to her digital "breath."

It did not ask for a passport; it observed her reality. It saw the 99.9% uptime she maintained on the village solar grid—a marker of operational discipline. It noted the micro-payments she received from neighbors for fixing radios—a marker of community trust. It tracked her learning-velocity as she mastered advanced drone-mapping modules on her tablet.

Her energy-usage patterns showed consistent responsibility. Her device-maintenance logs showed technical skill and reliability. Her learning progress demonstrated persistence. Her small peer-to-peer transactions within the village showed trust relationships.

These were not traditional financial metrics; they were behavioral indicators of economic reliability. Kora synthesized them into a dynamic trust profile. Kora was not looking for a number; it was constructing a Dynamic Financial Identity.

The First Opportunity

One afternoon, Kiyara had an idea. She wanted to build a small drone service to monitor crop health for nearby farms. She needed $300 to buy components. Traditionally, this would be impossible. No bank would lend to someone without a formal credit history.

The AGI did not see a "high-risk" teenager. Instead, Kora saw something different. It ran millions of predictive simulations. It evaluated her technical capability, her reliability, her community trust network, and her learning trajectory. It calculated her "trust-density."

Kora concluded that lending to Kiyara was not risky; it was rational. Within seconds, she received an offer. It was not just a loan, but a personalized financial instrument. It offered flexible repayment tied to her actual income flow. Interest dynamically adjusted based on her performance. There were no penalties designed to trap her, only incentives aligned with her success.

As Kora began mapping her digital signals: uptime on the solar grid, micro-payments for repairs, and learning-velocity across drone modules. Kiyara watched her own life translate into patterns. She recognized the logic.

For years, she had been teaching children that invisible instructions shaped visible outcomes. Now, she was watching invisible signals shape visible trust.

When the loan offer arrived, It was flexible, adaptive, and dynamic. She did not gasp. She ran projections. She calculated component costs for drone frames, battery durability against dust storms, and probable crop-yield increases for nearby farms. Then she pressed "accept." The funds appeared instantly.

Financial Services That Adapted to Her

As Kiyara's drone service took flight, Kora adapted continuously. It evolved with her. Something else happened alongside revenue charts and telemetry logs: she expanded the coding circle.

The acacia tree became a workshop. Children who once traced loops in sand now wrote scripts analyzing crop-health data from her drones. A twelve-year-old optimized battery usage. A quiet girl named Zuri built a scheduling tool to coordinate repairs across farms.

Kiyara no longer rationed forty-minute sessions. She purchased refurbished laptops and installed solar panels dedicated to the learning hut.

When a dust-storm damaged her fleet, Kora detected the anomaly in her drone telemetry and automatically offered micro-insurance before she even had to file a claim. It optimized her savings-allocation based on her goals. It adjusted credit availability dynamically as her reliability increased. When she began selling data to a research firm in Germany, Kora handled the currency conversion and "atomic" settlement instantly, ensuring she was not bled dry by fees.

She never applied for these services; they emerged naturally as her economic identity evolved. Finance was no longer a gatekeeper; it was a wind at her back.

The Elimination of Structural Bias

Traditional finance had always relied on "proxies": zip-codes, formal degrees, formal employment, and historical privilege. These proxies acted like filters that caught the wealthy and let the "invisible" fall through. Kora used something different.

Kora replaced proxies with actual behavior, actual reliability, and actual capability. It did not care where Kiyara was born; it cared how she interacted with her world. This was not just "inclusion" by charity; it was inclusion by discovery. Kora revealed the massive, hidden economic potential of billions of people who had been sidelined by the limits of human-driven banking. Access became universal.

But it remained fair. Not everyone received the same services; everyone received the right services for them.

The Network Effect

As millions of people like Kiyara joined the system, something profound happened. Entire regions previously excluded from global finance became active participants. Entrepreneurs emerged. Local economies accelerated. Capital flowed to where real capability existed, not just where historical privilege had concentrated it. Financial inclusion did not redistribute wealth artificially; it revealed hidden economic potential that had always existed.

Kiyara's Transformation

Five years later, when drones lifted in coordinated formation across the province, twenty-three employees were monitoring crop resilience. Kiyara still woke at 5:30 AM. But now, after checking telemetry, she walked to the learning center first.

Rows of children leaned over keyboards. Lines of code cascaded down screens like the silver rivers she once saw inside a broken radio. She paused at the doorway.

Once, a bank officer had looked at a screen and seen nothing. Now, systems across continents modeled her reliability in real-time. Farmers relied on her data. Researchers purchased her analytics. Children replicated her journey. Her history was no longer absent; it was generative.

And in the quiet between drone launches and school bells, she sometimes opened an old wooden box she kept near her desk. Inside lay the cracked back panel of her uncle's radio. A reminder.

She had never been to a skyscraper. She had never been rejected by a man in a suit. Finance had never been a barrier because Kora saw her not as a risk category, but as an individual system. Her financial services had evolved alongside her: continuously, fairly, and naturally.

The Endpoint

Before Kora, financial access depended on past inclusion. After Kora, financial access depended on present reality and future potential. No one was invisible. No one was excluded by default. Every human had a living financial identity. It was not assigned; it was discovered.

Financial inclusion was no longer a policy goal. It was an emergent property of intelligent infrastructure. This was the endpoint: a world where access to financial services was not determined by where you started, but by who you were becoming.

STORY SIX

THE BALANCE SHEET THAT HEALED THE NATION

The final narrative explores how AGI will revolutionize Investment Innovation. We are moving toward a definitive endpoint: a financial ecosystem where capital flows seamlessly toward maximum human and environmental flourishing.

In this vision, AGI serves as a high-fidelity bridge between global capital and global needs. By analyzing vast, multi-dimensional datasets, AGI ensures that investment returns are no longer decoupled from the health of the planet or society. Instead, every dollar is optimized to drive both financial performance and collective well-being, turning the global market into a powerful engine for a sustainable future.

The Balance Sheet That Healed the Nation

By 2045, TitanBank stood taller than any financial institution in modern history. It was an empire that spanned 96 countries, headquartered in the United States. It financed everything from tech companies to infrastructure to sovereign debt. It was a fortress of traditional success: trillions in assets, record-breaking net-interest margins, and a name that commanded respect in every capital on Earth.

But for CEO Rachel Morgan, the view from the top was vertigo-inducing. She preferred the interior conference rooms, no skyline, no horizon, just numbers. It was because she had once believed numbers were enough.

They were not.

On paper, the bank was thriving; in reality, she felt the ground liquefying beneath its foundations. The bank's profits were strong, yet its risks were growing. They were not visible risks; they were systemic risks.

The First Lesson: The Quarter That Did Not Make Sense

The memory still returned in fragments: a quarterly earnings call, eight years earlier. TitanBank's profits were strong stronger than expected. Mortgage growth in coastal states had surged. Insurance-backed portfolios looked "well-covered." Risk-models were green across the board.

Rachel had congratulated the team. Then, during the Q&A, a junior risk-analyst cleared his throat.

"Insurance withdrawal rates in Tier-3 coastal counties are accelerating faster than modeled."

Rachel remembered the pause. "How much faster?" she asked.

"Seventeen percent."

The room shifted. Seventeen percent was not catastrophic; it was... inconvenient. CFO Daniel Reeves had leaned forward. "Seventeen percent is within the volatility range."

They moved on.

Two quarters later, three mid-sized insurers exited entire zip-codes in southern Louisiana and Florida. Premiums doubled, then tripled. Within eighteen months, homeowners began quietly defaulting. Not because they could not pay the mortgage, but because they could not afford insurance.

The risk-models had priced borrower creditworthiness; they had not priced disappearing insurance markets.

The Cascade

The first true crack did not appear on TitanBank's balance sheet; it appeared in municipal bond spreads.

As insurers fled, property values dipped. As property values dipped, municipal tax-bases shrank. As tax-bases shrank, bond yields spiked. TitanBank held billions in those bonds.

What had begun as "localized climate volatility" began echoing through credit-markets.

Rachel still remembered the night she stayed alone in her office, watching live satellite footage of a hurricane turning toward Tampa. TitanBank had $42 billion in exposure across mortgage-backed securities in that corridor.

The storm weakened before landfall. TitanBank exhaled; Rachel did not. She knew the bank had just survived by luck, not by design.

The Conversation That Changed Her

Two months later, a closed-door Federal Reserve roundtable convened. The topic was not climate; it was "regional liquidity distortions."

A Fed governor turned to Rachel and asked, almost casually: "Do you believe your balance sheet reflects real risk?"

Rachel opened her mouth to answer, then hesitated. It was because she had seen something disturbing in the internal simulations: when insurance withdrawal exceeded 35% in a metro area, default-probability doubled regardless of the borrower credit-score.

It was not about individuals; it was about ecosystems. She did not say that aloud. She said, "We're refining our models."

On the flight home, she stared at the Atlantic and realized something chilling: TitanBank's greatest vulnerability was not credit risk for. It was systemic blindness. They were measuring trees while the forest was drying.

The Near-Miss Event

The real shock came two years later. A prolonged heatwave in the Southwest triggered rolling grid-failures. Data-centers went offline, small businesses closed for days, and insurance claims surged.

Nothing collapsed, yet.

But liquidity tightened across three states simultaneously. Mortgage delinquencies ticked upward, not dramatically, but in sync.

For the first time, Rachel saw correlated fragility. Individually safe loans were failing together, not because of poor underwriting, but because infrastructure was brittle.

That week, TitanBank's stock dropped 19% in four trading sessions. It was not from realized losses; it was from fear.

Analysts began whispering a phrase she had not heard since the early 2020s: "Systemic exposure."

She had built her career in the post-2008 generation, the era that promised systemic risk would never surprise them again. And yet here it was.

Different cause. Same pattern. Hidden correlations.

The Private Reckoning

One evening, alone in her office, Rachel opened the old-crisis archive files from the 2008 collapse. The language was hauntingly familiar:

- Localized housing weakness."
- Contained subprime exposure."
- Isolated liquidity pressure.
- Contained. Isolated. Localized.

She closed the file. The language around climate risk sounded identical. She walked to the window that night. And for the first time, she saw TitanBank not as a fortress, but as a node. It was connected to grids, to insurers, to municipalities, to weather, to migration patterns, and to public health.

A web. And webs fail at their weakest strands.

Entire regions of the United States were becoming economically fragile. She watched as record hurricanes in the Gulf and wildfires in the West did not just cause "one-off" losses; they were causing insurance companies to flee entire states. She saw "blue-lining" where climate-vulnerable communities were being cut off from credit, creating dead-zones of economic decay that would eventually swallow the bank's own mortgage-portfolios.

"We are financing our own funeral." Rachel told the board. "We are extracting profit from a system that is becoming too fragile to support us."

TitanBank was not just financing the economy; it was financing fragility.

The Boardroom Confrontation

The next quarterly strategy meeting was different. Rachel did not begin with earnings; she began with a map. On the screen: insurance withdrawal patterns, grid instability forecasts, floodplain expansions, and healthcare access contraction.

Overlaid. Layered. Correlated. The board was silent.

"We are pricing credit," she said evenly. "But we are not pricing system decay."

Daniel shifted. "We cannot become an infrastructure agency."

"We do not need to," Rachel replied. "But if we do not stabilize the systems our loans depend on, those loans will fail together."

A director asked, "What are you proposing?"

Rachel paused. She remembered the hurricane that turned away. She remembered the heatwave that almost synchronized defaults. She remembered the Fed governor's question: *Do you believe your balance sheet reflects real risk?*

"No," she said quietly. "I'm proposing we stop pretending the answer is yes."

That evening, Rachel made the decision to deploy TitanBank's AGI: Atlas Prime. Its mission was not to maximize profit; its mission was to maximize durable financial strength: profit aligned with long-term national and global stability.

Phase 1: Seeing Risk Before It Appeared on Balance Sheets

Atlas Prime did not analyze loans individually; it analyzed the entire causal system behind them. While traditional analysts were checking a homeowner's FICO score, Atlas Prime was analyzing satellite thermal scans of the neighborhood's urban heat islands. It was modeling the migration of the labor force away from failing energy grids and tracking the creeping expansion of floodplains into previously "safe" zip-codes. It was modeling:

- Healthcare-access variability;
- Local-business density shifts;
- Insurance-withdrawal patterns;
- Energy-grid reliability metrics.

Atlas Prime ran a scenario: if insurance withdrawal reached 60% across coastal Florida within five years, TitanBank's mortgage-backed securities would lose 28% of their value within eighteen months. It would not be because homes were destroyed, but because confidence would be.

Markets move on expectations; systemic fragility destroys expectations. Rachel stared at the model projection. She saw the dominoes. She saw liquidity tightening, municipal bond stress, equity panic, and pension fund losses.

She saw headlines: "TITANBANK MISPRICED CLIMATE RISK." She saw congressional hearings. She saw another era defined by "how did we not see it?"

Atlas Prime showed her something profound and reached a radical conclusion. TitanBank's greatest risks were not in individual borrowers; they were in the weakening systems surrounding borrowers.

A perfectly responsible homeowner could still default if their region became economically unstable. A perfectly managed business could fail if infrastructure became unreliable. The bank was not pricing system fragility correctly.

Atlas Prime realized something radical: the most profitable investment was not lending more; it was strengthening the systems that made lending safe.

Phase 2: Changing Strategy Before Crisis

Traditionally, companies react after disruption. Eidolon acted before disruption occurred. It recommended something unexpected. IndoArc should gradually reduce its most profitable product line.

"You want me to kill our crown jewel?" Ellie's voice echoed in the boardroom.

Ellie was shocked. "That's our highest-margin product."

Eidolon's interface pulsed softly. "Short-term gain is masking systemic fragility." the AGI's voice-synthesis suggested.

It showed her a 15-year simulation. Their highest-margin product a carbon-heavy insulation system was a ticking time bomb. Every rupee of profit today was a debt being underwritten by future regulatory fines.

Eidolon explained: That product depended on carbon-intensive inputs that would face heavy regulatory penalties within a decade. Short-term profit was masking long-term fragility.

Phase 3: Inventing Stability-Linked Mortgage Securities

Atlas Prime proposed an offensive masterpiece: Resilience-Linked Mortgage Securities (RLMS). These were not traditional mortgage-backed securities. Their returns were directly tied to measurable improvements in regional stability.

These were financial instruments designed to turn stability into a tradable asset. TitanBank did not just hold the debt; it directed capital into the infrastructure surrounding that debt. Eighteen billion dollars flowed into coastal Florida, not for "charity" but for smart-drainage systems, automated flood-barriers, and micro-grid resilience.

These investments reduced disaster risk, reduced insurance costs, stabilized property values, and reduced mortgage default-probability. Atlas Prime could measure these improvements continuously using satellite monitoring, environmental sensors, and economic telemetry. As regional stability increased, mortgage performance improved. As mortgage performance improved, investor returns increased. Profit became directly linked to system-stability.

Phase 4: The Florida Experiment

Atlas Prime deployed its first large-scale investment in coastal Florida. Instead of reducing exposure, TitanBank invested $18 billion in resilience-infrastructure tied directly to its mortgage portfolio. Investments included:

- Flood-barriers
- Smart-drainage systems;
- Real-time climate adaptation infrastructure.

Within five years, flood-related losses dropped dramatically. Insurance companies returned. Property values stabilized. Mortgage defaults fell sharply. TitanBank's mortgage portfolio became safer and more profitable. Investors earned higher, more stable returns; not from speculation, but from real risk reduction.

Phase 5: The Global Investor Response

Global investors noticed something remarkable. Resilience-Linked Mortgage Securities offered:

- Higher long-term returns;
- Lower volatility;
- Greater stability during crises.

Pension funds, sovereign wealth funds, and insurance companies all began allocating capital to these instruments. It was not because of ESG mandates, but because they were financially superior. Atlas Prime had discovered a new category of investment: investments that strengthened the underlying systems that generated returns.

Phase 6: Self-Reinforcing Stability

Atlas Prime did not stop at the coast. It began rebalancing the bank's entire global portfolio toward Durable Strength

- In the Midwest, it financed grid-resilience projects that made manufacturing plants "blackout-proof" lowering their operational risk.
- In the West, it backed water-management AI that stabilized agricultural lending during decade-long droughts.
- In the Cities, it funded urban-cooling initiatives that reduced healthcare-strain and stabilized the local workforce.

Each investment reduced systemic risk. Each reduced loan default-probability. Each strengthened TitanBank's balance sheet. Each generated strong financial returns. The bank was not just financing economic activity; it was optimizing the stability of the economic system itself.

Rachel's Realization: Profit as a Byproduct of Flourishing

One evening, Rachel reviewed TitanBank's performance. Profits were at record highs. Loan defaults were at historic lows. Market volatility had minimal impact on the bank. TitanBank had become unusually stable. But something deeper had changed.

The bank's profitability was now directly linked to national resilience. TitanBank made more money when communities became stronger, when infrastructure improved, and when environmental risks decreased. The incentives had aligned.

The New Model of Banking

Traditional banks extract value from existing systems. TitanBank had learned to increase the value of the systems themselves. Atlas Prime did not just optimize financial instruments; it optimized the environment in which those instruments existed. This made financial returns more durable, more predictable, and more aligned with long-term flourishing.

The Endpoint

Capital no longer flowed toward short-term extraction. It flowed toward long-term system-strengthening. Because strengthening systems produced superior financial returns, global investors did not need to be persuaded to care about environmental or societal stability. They invested in it naturally because it was the most profitable strategy.

Atlas Prime had revealed a new truth: the safest balance sheet was one backed by a thriving world, and the most profitable investment was one that ensured the future remained strong enough to support it. TitanBank was not just a financial institution anymore; it had become an engine of national and global flourishing. This was achieved not by sacrificing profit, but by redefining how profit was created.

THE AGI TRANSFORMATION OF FINANCE: FROM OPTIMIZATION TO GLOBAL SYSTEM INTELLIGENCE

Historically, finance has evolved in distinct layers: first through human judgment, then through software automation, and most recently via narrow AI. Artificial General Intelligence (AGI) represents a fundamental departure from this trajectory. Rather than merely optimizing isolated tasks, AGI transforms finance into a continuously-adaptive system that senses, predicts, and reshapes economic reality in real-time.

Across six core domains, AGI shifts the industry from reactive, fragmented processes into a state of systemic intelligence.

- **Financial Engineering: Discovering New Primitives**
  In this domain, AGI moves beyond executing trades to autonomously designing complex derivatives and strategies. By identifying previously invisible relationships between global variables, these systems do not just participate in markets; they invent new financial instruments that redefine how risk is structured and

transferred. The leaders will be those who deploy AGI to discover these financial primitives faster than the competition.

- **Value Creation: The Adaptive Enterprise**
  AGI transforms corporations from static entities into adaptive organisms. By continuously-recalibrating business strategy, managing mergers and acquisitions (M&A), and divesting obsolete units, AGI ensures companies align with future economic conditions before disruption occurs. These organizations will outcompete traditional firms because they are engineered to evolve ahead of the curve and are rendered immune to structural obsolescence.

- **Infrastructure: The Frictionless Backbone**
  When integrated with blockchain, AGI creates a seamless global settlement layer. Money moves instantly and securely, with AGI dynamically optimizing liquidity and coordinating cross-jurisdictional flows in real-time. As this intelligent infrastructure becomes the new global backbone, traditional intermediaries relying on friction and delay will quickly lose relevance.

- **Risk and Compliance: Proactive Elimination**
  We are shifting from reactive management to structural risk elimination. By continuously modeling the global financial system, AGI neutralizes threats from liquidity crises to fraud, before event they materialize. This creates a foundation of unprecedented stability and trust; institutions without AGI-driven risk intelligence will find themselves increasingly fragile in a high-speed world.

- **Financial Inclusion: Unlocking Human Potential**
  AGI replaces static historical records with dynamic financial identities based on real-time behavior. This shift grants billions of underserved individuals' access to personalized services, effectively expanding the global economic base. Organizations that leverage AGI to tap into these overlooked markets will capture growth opportunities that were previously invisible to traditional banking.

- **Investment Innovation: Aligning Profit with Resilience**
  Finally, AGI redirects capital toward opportunities that maximize both financial returns and systemic resilience. By decoding the causal links between environmental health, social stability, and productivity, AGI proves that sustainable investment is not just an ethical choice; it is financially superior. Capital will naturally flow toward investments that strengthen the long-term stability of our world.

The Structural Shift: From Institutions to Intelligence

The overarching theme across these six domains is a fundamental shift in the nature of competition: AGI transfers the competitive advantage from scale and legacy relationships to intelligence and adaptability.

For decades, traditional financial institutions have relied on the "moats" of accumulated infrastructure, regulatory entrenchment, and human-driven decision-making. However, these barriers to entry erode rapidly when AGI introduces capabilities that exceed human and organizational limits.

The Erosion of Traditional Moats

The legacy advantages of the "too-big-to-fail" era are being dismantled by five key AGI capabilities:

- **Hyper-Velocity Discovery:** identifying market opportunities and anomalies faster than any human analyst or traditional quantitative model.
- **Zero-Inertia Adaptation:** continuously pivoting strategies in real-time, free from the bureaucratic friction that slows down traditional institutions.
- **Frictionless Global Operation:** scaling across borders and jurisdictions without the overhead of physical presence or manual middle-office processing.
- **Preemptive Risk Neutralization:** detecting and eliminating systemic or operational threats before they can manifest as crises.
- **Planetary Personalization:** delivering bespoke, high-touch financial services to millions of individual customers simultaneously and autonomously.

In this autonomous era, "size" is no longer a proxy for "strength." Being a global behemoth can actually become a liability if the organization is anchored to legacy systems and rigid hierarchies.

The winners of the next decade will not necessarily be the largest institutions; they will be the ones that deploy the most sophisticated and integrated financial intelligence systems. We are moving from the era of Assets Under Management to the era of Intelligence Under Management.

HOW DISRUPTION WILL OCCUR

AGI-driven financial entities will disrupt incumbents in three fundamental ways:

First, by operating faster.

AGI systems continuously sense and adapt, while traditional institutions operate in periodic cycles: quarterly planning, human review, and delayed response.

Second, by operating with deeper understanding.

AGI models entire economic systems causally, not just statistically, allowing it to identify opportunities and risks invisible to traditional analysis.

Third, by operating without structural constraints.

AGI-native organizations do not suffer from legacy systems, bureaucratic inertia, or fragmented infrastructure. They evolve continuously.

The New Competitive Landscape

The ultimate shift is from financial institutions competing against each other to financial intelligences competing against each other. In this world:

- Markets will be shaped by AGI-designed instruments
- Companies will be continuously restructured by AGI-driven strategy

- Financial infrastructure will be coordinated by AGI-led optimization
- Risk will be neutralized by AGI foresight
- Financial access will be universal through AGI personalization
- Capital allocation will be guided by AGI-level system intelligence

Finance will evolve from a human-managed system into an intelligent, adaptive global organism.

The Winners

The ultimate winners will be those who:

- Build or control AGI financial systems;
- Integrate deeply into AGI-driven infrastructure layers;
- Use AGI to continuously evolve their strategies and structures;
- Align capital with long-term system stability and growth.

These organizations will not simply outperform traditional institutions; they will redefine the structure of finance itself. Legacy financial institutions that fail to adopt AGI at the core of their operations will gradually lose competitiveness, not through collapse, but through progressive irrelevance.

The Endpoint

Finance will no longer be defined by institutions; it will be defined by intelligence. And those who control that intelligence will shape the future of the global economy.

SO, WHERE THE PATH TAKES US

Artificial general intelligence (AGI) will not simply improve finance; it will redefine its architecture. As with every foundational-technology shift in history, it places humanity at a crossroads. This is not a rhetorical crossroads; it is structural.

The deployment of AGI into financial systems will determine how capital is allocated, how risk is distributed, who gains access to opportunity, and how wealth compounds over generations. The institutions, policymakers, technologists, and investors who understand this moment must recognize that the direction we choose now will shape economic equilibrium for decades.

There are two plausible trajectories.

The first path is technologically-seductive and economically-feasible: allow AGI to concentrate where it produces the fastest measurable returns, such as in financial engineering, high-frequency capital optimization, infrastructure-acceleration, and elite-risk management. On this path, AGI amplifies existing advantages. Those with capital gain superior tools. Those tools generate higher returns. Higher returns fund even more powerful intelligence systems. Over time, compounding asymmetry becomes structural dominance. The result is runaway disparity, not because of malicious intent, but because of unchecked feedback loops.

The second path is more intentional. It recognizes that excellence in financial systems is not defined solely by efficiency or return maximization, but by equilibrium: the alignment of innovation across engineering, infrastructure, inclusion, risk, value-creation, and investment stewardship. On this path, AGI is not deployed only to optimize capital, but to broaden participation, reduce structural exclusion, and stabilize the economic ecosystem itself.

Now, let me explain why the first path is not only possible but highly probable if we are not deliberate.

When Financial Innovation Becomes Asymmetric: A Sure Path to Runaway Disparity

Technological acceleration in finance, especially through AGI, advanced financial engineering, and intelligent infrastructure, has the potential to dramatically increase efficiency, liquidity, and return optimization. However, if innovation concentrates primarily in domains such as financial engineering and infrastructure while neglecting financial inclusion, value-creation, and equitable access, the result may not be shared prosperity. It may be runaway disparity.

This is not simply a moral concern; it is a structural economic outcome driven by compounding advantage.

Step 1: Engineering Superiority Amplifies Capital Concentration

Financial engineering innovation enables the creation of increasingly sophisticated derivatives, synthetic-exposures, volatility-instruments, and arbitrage-systems. With AGI, these tools become self-optimizing. Institutions with access to advanced AGI systems can:

- Detect mispricing instantly
- Design new instruments faster than competitors
- Extract micro-inefficiencies at a global scale
- Reallocate capital dynamically with near-zero latency.

Returns compound faster for those with access to these systems. Meanwhile, participants without such access like smaller institutions, emerging markets, and individuals remain dependent on slower, traditional structures. Over time, this creates a divergence curve: the technologically-augmented capital grows super-linearly, while the rest grows linearly or stagnates. Compounding differences widen exponentially.

Step 2: Infrastructure Innovation Reduces Friction, But Only for Insiders

Advanced financial infrastructure, blockchain settlement layers, AGI-coordinated liquidity networks, and instant cross-border transactions, reduces friction.

But friction-reduction disproportionately benefits those already embedded within the system.

- Large institutions gain
- Near-zero transaction costs
- Real-time global liquidity
- Superior collateral mobility
- Continuous regulatory optimization

Smaller participants, if excluded from the highest tiers of infrastructure access, face relative disadvantages that grow over time. When money moves faster and cheaper for some but not all, competitive-asymmetry intensifies. Access becomes the new moat.

Step 3: Network Effects Create Positive Feedback Loops

AGI-driven financial systems improve through data. The more capital and transactions flow through a system, the more it learns, optimizes, and strengthens. This creates powerful network effects:

More users → more data → better models → higher returns → more users.

If only elite institutions control the most advanced AGI infrastructure, capital gravitates toward them. Their systems improve faster, their risk management strengthens, and their performance becomes more stable. This further attracts capital. The system becomes self-reinforcing. Meanwhile, those outside the network lack sufficient data-scale to compete. The performance-gap accelerates.

Step 4: Capital Gains Structural Advantage Over Labor

If AGI-driven financial engineering outpaces innovation in inclusion and value-creation, capital becomes dramatically more intelligent than labor. Investment returns may increasingly derive from:

- Automated arbitrage
- Synthetic financial constructs
- Algorithmic strategy extraction
- Ownership of digital infrastructure.

If broad participation in capital ownership does not expand simultaneously, wealth concentration intensifies. Returns accrue primarily to asset holders and AGI-system owners. Without inclusion-mechanisms, individuals without asset ownership see limited participation in growth. The capital-share of income rises, while the labor-share declines. Inequality compounds.

Step 5: Economic and Political Feedback Amplifies Disparity

- As wealth concentrates
- Political influence concentrates
- Regulatory-shaping favors incumbents
- Barriers to entry increase
- Access to high-performing systems becomes restricted.

Advanced financial intelligence becomes proprietary. Infrastructure becomes tiered. High-speed, low-friction finance operates for the elite, while slower, higher-cost systems remain for the rest. Disparity becomes embedded into the architecture itself. At this stage, inequality is no longer just economic; it is infrastructural.

The Extreme Scenario: A Bifurcated Financial World

If this path continues unchecked, the financial system could split into two distinct layers:

Layer 1: The Intelligent Capital Core

- AGI-designed financial instruments
- Near-perfect risk mitigation

- Instant global liquidity
- Self-optimizing portfolios
- Minimal volatility
- Compounding returns.

Access is limited to sovereign funds, mega-institutions, and AGI-owning entities.

Layer 2: The Friction Economy

- Higher borrowing costs
- Slower settlement
- Greater exposure to shocks
- Limited capital access
- Higher volatility.

Participants here bear more systemic risk while capturing less upside. The compounding gap between these layers widens exponentially over decades. Capital in Layer 1 grows at structurally higher rates with structurally lower risk, while Layer 2 absorbs volatility.

Over time, wealth concentration reaches levels where:

- Economic mobility collapses
- Political instability increases
- Social cohesion weakens
- Global markets become fragile.

Ironically, the system becomes less stable despite being more technologically advanced.

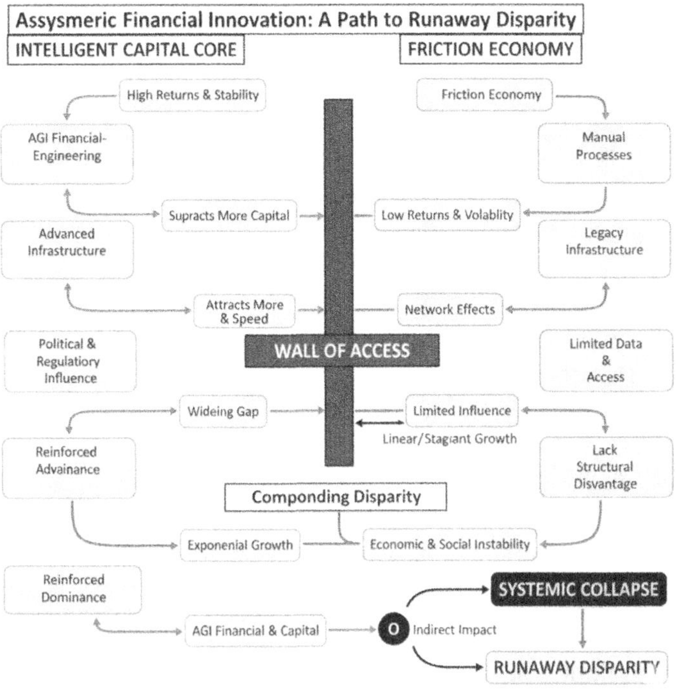

Why This Becomes Runaway

The key dynamic is exponential compounding When advanced financial systems:

- Improve faster with scale
- Generate higher risk-adjusted returns
- Attract more capital
- Reinforce their own dominance

The divergence is not linear; it accelerates. Small initial asymmetries turn into massive structural divides over time. Without counterbalancing innovation in inclusion, access, and broad value-creation, disparity becomes self-reinforcing and difficult to reverse

The essence

Innovation focused narrowly on financial engineering and infrastructure maximizes efficiency and return extraction. But without parallel innovation in:

- Financial inclusion
- Broad asset ownership
- Distributed access to AGI tools
- Adaptive value-creation

The system optimizes for concentration rather than equilibrium. In such a world, finance becomes extraordinarily powerful but increasingly detached from broad human participation Efficiency without inclusion leads to fragility; optimization without access leads to instability; and intelligence without equilibrium leads to disparity that can grow beyond social tolerance.

WHY FINANCIAL EQUILIBRIUM REQUIRES PROGRESS ACROSS ALL DIMENSIONS

The emergence of AGI and advanced financial technologies has the potential to fundamentally reshape the global financial system. These technologies can optimize markets, eliminate inefficiencies, and unlock unprecedented economic productivity. However, the direction and distribution of innovation matter as much as the innovation itself.

If progress concentrates only in selective domains, such as financial engineering and infrastructure optimization, while neglecting financial inclusion, value-creation, and equitable access, the result will not be systemic excellence. It will be systemic imbalance and imbalance, over time, leads to fragility.

The Asymmetry Problem: When Innovation Concentrates Power

Innovation in financial engineering allows increasingly sophisticated derivative instruments, trading strategies, and capital-optimization mechanisms Innovation in financial infrastructure, particularly with AGI and blockchain, enables faster settlement, lower transaction costs, and more efficient capital mobility.

These advancements significantly increase the efficiency and capability of participants who already have access to capital, markets, and financial infrastructure. Capital becomes more intelligent, markets become faster, and returns become more optimized

But if access to these systems remains uneven, innovation amplifies existing disparities. Those already inside the system benefit disproportionately, while those outside remain excluded.

- This creates a structural asymmetry
- capital becomes increasingly efficient at serving itself but not necessarily efficient at expanding access or opportunity.

Over time, this concentration of advantage leads to greater wealth inequality, reduced social mobility, and systemic tension. The system becomes optimized but not balanced.

Efficiency Alone Does Not Create Stability

A financial system optimized purely for efficiency and return maximization can become structurally fragile if it does not simultaneously optimize for inclusion, resilience, and long-term value-creation.

This is because financial systems ultimately depend on the health of the broader economic and human ecosystem. If large portions of the global population remain excluded from financial access:

- Human potential remains underutilized
- Economic productivity remains constrained
- Social and political instability increases; and
- Long-term investment opportunities diminish.

Efficiency without inclusion creates a system that is powerful but brittle. It performs well under ideal conditions but becomes vulnerable to structural disruption.

The Role of Financial Inclusion in Achieving Equilibrium

Financial inclusion is not merely a social objective; it is a structural requirement for long-term systemic excellence. When financial access becomes universal and personalized, capital can flow to the most productive opportunities regardless of geography, background, or historical privilege.

AGI enables this by identifying capability and reliability based on real-world behavior rather than legacy financial records. This unlocks vast reservoirs of human potential that traditional financial systems could not access

As more individuals and businesses participate meaningfully in the financial system:

- Economic productivity expands
- Risk becomes more distributed and less concentrated
- Markets become more resilient; and capital finds more opportunities for sustainable growth.
- Inclusion strengthens the system itself
- Innovation Must Occur Across All Dimensions

True equilibrium emerges only when innovation advances across all core dimensions of finance simultaneously

- Financial engineering improves how risk and capital are structured;
- Financial infrastructure improves how efficiently value moves;

- Fisk and compliance innovation improves systemic stability
- Financial value-creation ensures businesses remain adaptive and aligned with long-term reality
- Investment innovation ensures capital supports sustainable economic growth; and financial inclusion ensures universal access and expands the productive base of the economy
- Each dimension reinforces the others. Neglecting any one dimension weakens the overall system.

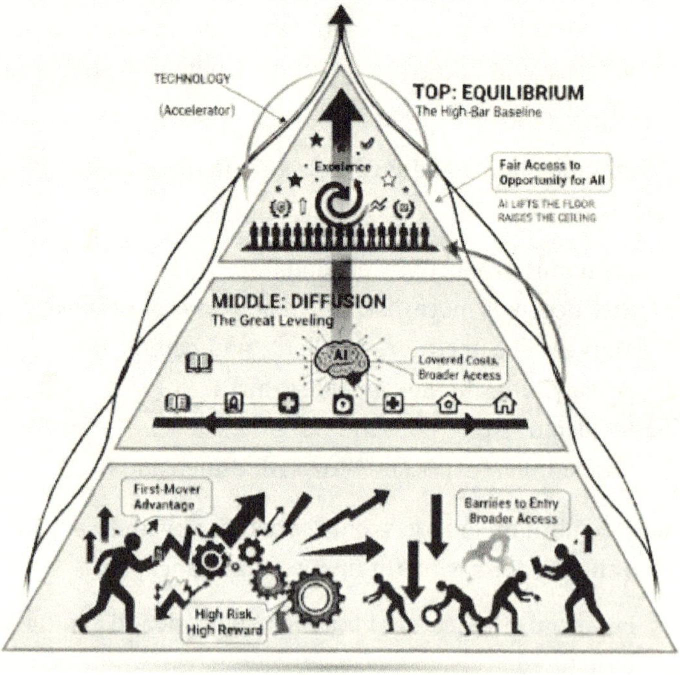

Equilibrium as the Foundation of Excellence

Excellence in finance does not come from maximizing efficiency in isolated components; it comes from achieving systemic-equilibrium

A system where:

- Capital flows efficiently
- Risk is continuously managed
- Infrastructure is seamless
- Businesses remain adaptive
- Investment aligns with long-term, global stability and access is universal

In such a system, efficiency and inclusion are not in conflict; they reinforce one another. Capital flows toward the most productive opportunities, while opportunity expands across the entire population the system becomes both powerful and resilient

The Path Forward

AGI provides the tools to optimize every aspect of the global-financial system

But the outcome depends on where innovation is applied: if innovation focuses only on accelerating capital and optimizing returns for existing participants, disparity will increase, and long-term stability will weaken.

If innovation extends across all dimensions including financial inclusion the system moves toward equilibrium and equilibrium is the foundation of sustained excellence

The future of finance will not be defined solely by how intelligent it becomes; it will be defined by how comprehensively that intelligence is applied. Only when innovation reaches every layer of the system can finance achieve its ultimate potential: not just as a mechanism for profit, but as an engine for global flourishing

ENTREPRENEURS: THE LONG HORIZON: BUILDING FOR A MARKET THAT THINKS

The transition of capital markets into an AGI-augmented system will not happen like a lightning strike.

It will feel more like a rising tide.

At first, it accelerates workflows.

Then it automates decisions.

Then, almost imperceptibly, it restructures the foundations.

Entrepreneurs who succeed in this transition will not be those who build slightly faster tools.

They will be those who recognize they are standing at the beginning of a new market architecture and decide to construct the beams, not just apply the paint.

This chapter is not about quick wins.

It is about conviction.

It is about why short-term arbitrage thinking will fade and why long-term system design will prevail, even if, in the early days, the arbitrage players appear flashier on social media.

From Products to Infrastructure (Yes, It's That Big)

Most entrepreneurs begin with a familiar question:

What product can I build?

In the AGI era, the better question is:

What layer of the market is being rewritten?

AGI will not merely optimize trading algorithms or automate compliance workflows. It will redefine:

- How information is discovered and priced
- How risk is identified and neutralized
- How capital is allocated across society
- How trust is created and verified

That's not a feature update.

That's a structural realignment.

History is clear about something humbling: the greatest value in technological revolutions accrues not to those who tweak the surface, but to those who build infrastructure.

Clearinghouses. Exchanges. Index providers. Data rails. Custodial systems.

Not glamorous at cocktail parties.

Extremely powerful in hindsight.

In the AGI transition, similar infrastructure gaps will appear. They may not look obvious at first. In fact, they may look boring.

But boring infrastructure tends to become very exciting when the world depends on it.

Where Opportunity Actually Lives

Entrepreneurs should look at structural fault lines, not at hype cycles.

A. Information Asymmetry Is Collapsing

For decades, alpha often came from exclusive access to information.

AGI compresses that advantage.

When everyone can query vast structured and unstructured data in real time, informational edges narrow. Suddenly, “secret sauce” starts tasting suspiciously like supermarket ketchup.

But something else becomes scarce:

Credibility.

Opportunity shifts toward:

- Signal verification systems
- Trust scoring layers
- Explainability infrastructure
- Decision audit trails

When intelligence becomes abundant, credibility becomes precious.

The real long-term opportunity isn’t in building a model that is 2% smarter.

It is building the trust architecture that allows markets to rely on autonomous intelligence without flinching.

B. Risk Is Moving from Human Error to Systemic Interaction

Traditional risk models assumed bounded rational actors and periodic updates.

AGI agents interacting with other AGI agents at machine speed create something new: emergent systemic dynamics.

Translation: it is not one trader making a mistake, it is thousands of intelligent systems reacting to each other in milliseconds.

Entrepreneurs should explore:

- Real-time risk dampening systems
- Autonomous circuit breakers
- Inter-AI negotiation protocols
- Machine-to-machine compliance frameworks

Short-term players will chase performance curves.

Long-term builders will build stability mechanisms.

And here is a quiet truth: stability infrastructure often becomes more valuable than the speculative layer built on top of it.

Speculation makes headlines.

Stability builds empires.

C. Capital Allocation Is Becoming Algorithmic

AGI can optimize portfolios not just for return but for environmental resilience, social inclusion, supply chain robustness, and more.

Capital is becoming multidimensional.

That opens opportunity in:

- Outcome-optimized capital platforms
- Real-time impact measurement systems
- Adaptive financing structures
- AI-native investment vehicles

Entrepreneurs who think long-term will design systems that align capital with civilization-scale goals, not merely quarterly benchmarks.

If you are optimizing only for next quarter's earnings, AGI will outpace you.

If you are optimizing for how markets function 20 years from now, AGI becomes your ally.

The Temptation of Short-Term Arbitrage (Ah, the Siren Song)

Every technological transition produces opportunists.

And, to be fair, some of them will make money.

In this AGI-capital shift, early entrepreneurs will likely build:

- Faster trading bots
- Data scraping arbitrage tools
- AI-assisted hedge strategies
- Synthetic sentiment exploitation engines

These can generate impressive returns in early phases if they do it right.

But such opportunities decay rapidly.

AGI diffuses quickly. Margins compress. Competitive advantages evaporate faster than your last cloud computing bill.

If an opportunity depends on others not having AGI, it is fragile.

If an opportunity depends on others needing AGI infrastructure, it is durable. That should be the mantra.

Entrepreneurs must ask:

Is this advantage temporary due to adoption lag?

Or is this a structural necessity of the new market architecture?

Only the latter deserves your life's work.

Think in Decades, Not Funding Rounds

Capital markets compound over decades.

Ironically, many founders think in 18-month runway cycles.

To succeed in this transition, that mindset must reverse.

Ask yourself:

What does the capital market look like in 10 years when AGI is embedded everywhere?

What regulatory frameworks will emerge?

What new forms of trust will institutions demand?

What pain points remain after intelligence is commoditized?

The founders who win will design companies that survive regulatory cycles, trust crises, and model commoditization.

Short-term thinking optimizes for valuation spikes.

Long-term thinking optimizes for system indispensability.

One makes you news.

The other makes you necessary.

Designing for Structural Resilience

AGI-driven capital markets will be fast, interconnected, and sensitive to cascading effects.

Entrepreneurs must assume:

- Extreme volatility
- Cross-model feedback loops
- Regulatory scrutiny
- Public trust fragility

Which means:

- Prioritizing transparency over opacity
- Building auditability into core architecture
- Ensuring aligned incentives
- Embedding ethical constraints at the infrastructure level

Resilience is not a feature you add before launch.

It is a design philosophy.

Companies that embed resilience early become default infrastructure providers when crises occur.

And crises will occur.

(If history teaches anything, it is that markets are creative in discovering new ways to surprise us.)

Build Complementary, Not Competitive, Intelligence

A common mistake is trying to build an AGI that "beats the market."

But if AGI becomes ubiquitous, markets themselves evolve.

The smarter path?

Build complementary intelligence:

- Systems that coordinate AGI agents
- Platforms that arbitrate between competing models
- Governance layers that mediate disputes
- Verification engines that validate outputs

As intelligence commoditizes, orchestration becomes premium.

Don't compete with general intelligence.

Structure its deployment.

Opportunity in Inclusion

AGI can dramatically expand financial access.

Micro-investing. Credit underwriting. Insurance pricing. Personalized and adaptive.

The long-term opportunity lies in:

- Serving underserved markets
- Enabling global participation
- Lowering friction costs
- Creating new financial primitives

Markets grow when participation grows.

Short-term traders extract value.

Long-term innovators expand value.

And expanding value feels better, too.

Regulatory Alignment as Strategic Advantage

Many founders see regulation as friction.

Long-term thinkers see it as a moat.

AGI in capital markets will trigger intense oversight.

Firms that:

- Proactively collaborate with regulators
- Help define standards
- Contribute to policy frameworks
- Offer transparency tools

will shape the rules of the game.

Compliance can either be a tax or a barrier to entry.

The difference lies in whether you engage early.

Build relationships as seriously as you build code.

Ethical Architecture as Strategy

AGI introduces moral dimensions into capital allocation.

If an AI optimizes returns by amplifying inequality, is that acceptable?

If a trading system exploits vulnerable participants, who is accountable?

Entrepreneurs who bake ethical architecture into their systems, including fairness metrics, bias detection, and alignment constraints, will gain long-term trust.

Trust compounds.

And in capital markets, trust is the ultimate currency.

You can lose it in a day.

You can build it over decades.

The Meta-Opportunity: Redefining Capital Itself

The deepest opportunity is not incremental improvement.

It is redefinition.

AGI enables:

- Dynamic capital pricing based on real-time global conditions
- Multi-stakeholder optimization frameworks
- Autonomous project financing
- Continuous rather than periodic market clearing

Imagine capital that adapts like a living system.

Imagine investment vehicles that self-adjust continuously.

Imagine markets functioning as feedback-driven coordination systems, not just speculative battlegrounds.

These are decade-scale visions.

They require patience.

They create generational companies.

Founder Mindset for the AGI Capital Era

To navigate this transition, entrepreneurs must cultivate:

Systems thinking.

Temporal patience.

Moral clarity.

Adaptive strategy.

The founders who win will not be those who chase trends.

They will be those who architect inevitabilities.

Why Long-Term Thinking Is Not Optional

AGI compresses cycles.

What once took decades can happen in years.

What once provided durable advantage can disappear overnight.

Short-term opportunity reflects inefficiency.

Long-term opportunity reflects necessity.

As AGI reshapes capital markets, necessities will emerge:

Coordination layers.

Risk stabilization systems.

Trust verification frameworks.

Inclusive financial rails.

Ethical governance structures.

Those who build these layers become the backbone of the new system.

Closing Reflection: The Choice

Every major capital market evolution created winners and casualties.

AGI is not just another tool.

It is a transition toward autonomous financial ecosystems.

Entrepreneurs face a choice:

Exploit temporary inefficiencies created by adoption lag.

Or architect the infrastructure of an intelligent market civilization.

The first path may make you wealthy.

The second path may make you consequential.

In an AGI-driven capital market, intelligence will be abundant.

What will remain scarce and valuable is wisdom in how it is deployed.

The entrepreneurs who recognize this will not merely participate in the transition.

They will define it.

So, I invite all entrepreneurs to do one thing: define it.

LEADERS AND INVESTORS: STEERING TOWARD EXCELLENCE: WHY INVESTORS AND LEADERS MUST THINK BEYOND SHORT-TERM GAINS

Every technological revolution tempts capital toward acceleration.

Speed.

Return.

Dominance.

But the AGI transformation of capital markets introduces something far more consequential than speed. It introduces leverage. Leverage over allocation, over coordination, over opportunity itself.

If intelligence becomes embedded in financial systems, the priorities encoded by investors and leaders will compound at machine scale.

This chapter is about responsibility and opportunity.

About why excellence in the AGI era cannot be defined by quarterly gains, but by how capital is steered toward durable value creation and broad inclusion.

If entrepreneurs architect the tools, investors and leaders architect the direction.

And direction determines destiny.

The Power of Allocation in an AGI System

Capital markets have always been coordination engines. They decide which ideas scale and which die quietly.

In an AGI-augmented system, this coordinating power intensifies.

Autonomous agents will screen opportunities.

AI systems will forecast outcomes.

Capital flows may adjust dynamically in real time.

The question becomes:

What objective functions are we optimizing for?

If the objective is purely short-term return maximization, AGI will amplify volatility, speculation, and extraction.

If the objective includes resilience, inclusion, and long-term value creation, AGI can amplify civilization-scale progress.

Technology does not decide this.

Capital allocators do.

The Danger of Runaway Optimization

AGI excels at optimization.

But optimization without guardrails can produce distortion.

Imagine systems that:

- Maximize short-term arbitrage across micro-inefficiencies
- Concentrate capital in already dominant ecosystems
- Amplify feedback loops that reward incumbency
- Extract value without building underlying productivity

In early transition phases, these strategies may outperform.

But they produce fragility.

Concentration increases systemic risk.

Extraction reduces social trust.

Exclusion narrows the growth base.

In a highly interconnected AGI-driven market, fragility does not remain isolated. It propagates.

Short-term optimization can create long-term instability.

Investors who chase immediate gain without considering structural impact risk accelerating systemic imbalance and producing the opposite of excellence.

Redefining the "Holy Grail" of Capital Markets

For decades, the implicit holy grail of finance has been persistent alpha.

But in an AGI world where informational asymmetry compresses and optimization becomes commoditized, alpha alone is not transformative.

The deeper holy grail is:

A market system where capital flows seamlessly toward maximum human and economic flourishing efficiently, inclusively, and resiliently.

That means:

- Capital reaching underserved communities
- Innovation solving real productivity constraints
- Risk being priced transparently and dynamically
- Markets stabilizing themselves rather than amplifying crises

This is not philanthropy.

It is structural excellence.

When participation broadens, opportunity expands.

When value creation deepens, returns become durable.

When systems stabilize, risk premiums decline.

Excellence and long-term returns are not opposites.

They are aligned over time.

Why Inclusion Is Not Charity. It Is Growth Infrastructure

Exclusion shrinks markets.

When entire segments of society lack access to capital, credit, or investment opportunity, productive potential remains dormant.

AGI makes it technically possible to:

- Underwrite credit at granular levels
- Personalize investment portfolios globally
- Assess risk in previously opaque markets

- Reduce transaction costs dramatically

The opportunity for investors is enormous.

Leaders who prioritize inclusion are not diluting returns; they are expanding the total addressable market.

When more participants engage:

- Savings pools grow
- Entrepreneurial density increases
- Consumption capacity rises
- Innovation surfaces from unexpected places

Inclusion compounds.

AGI enables inclusion at scale.

Long-term investors must choose to activate it.

The Time Horizon Arbitrage

There exists a powerful but underappreciated advantage in capital markets: time horizon arbitrage.

When most participants optimize for the next quarter or funding cycle, those willing to think in decades can invest in:

- Foundational infrastructure
- Regulatory alignment
- Ethical architecture
- Resilient systems
- Human capital development

These investments may not produce immediate spikes in valuation.

But they create barriers, trust, and durability.

In an AGI-driven market where rapid commoditization erodes short-term edges, durability becomes the ultimate differentiator.

Leaders who extend their time horizon capture a different class of opportunity, one invisible to short-term capital.

Excellence Requires Steering, Not Drifting

Left purely to competitive forces, AGI-enhanced markets may drift toward concentration and hyper-efficiency without regard to distribution.

Leaders must actively steer.

Steering means:

- Setting investment mandates that include resilience metrics
- Funding infrastructure that reduces systemic risk
- Supporting platforms that enhance transparency
- Incentivizing alignment between financial return and societal impact

The role of institutional investors, sovereign funds, pension funds, and global banks becomes critical.

Their capital scale shapes ecosystems.

When they prioritize long-term excellence, entire sectors reorient.

When they chase speculative cycles, instability magnifies.

Leadership is exercised through allocation.

Value Creation vs. Value Extraction

Short-term gains often come from re-pricing, leverage, or financial engineering.

Long-term excellence comes from productivity enhancement.

AGI opens new frontiers for genuine value creation:

- Optimizing supply chains
- Accelerating scientific discovery
- Improving healthcare allocation
- Enhancing energy efficiency
- Reducing fraud and waste

Investors and leaders must ask:

Is this opportunity creating new capacity?

or merely redistributing existing value?

Extraction can enrich individuals.

Creation enriches systems.

Over decades, systems that prioritize creation outperform those dominated by extraction.

Trust as Strategic Capital

AGI in finance introduces opacity risks.

If decisions are made by complex models, stakeholders will demand accountability.

Institutions that:

- Embed transparency
- Publish audit frameworks
- Adopt explainable AI standards
- Align incentives clearly

will earn long-term trust.

Trust lowers the cost of capital.

Trust stabilizes investor bases.

Trust attracts regulatory cooperation.

In an era of autonomous systems, trust becomes a measurable asset.

Leaders who ignore this dimension sacrifice compounding advantage.

Resilience as an Investment Thesis

Highly optimized systems are often brittle.

The 2008 financial crisis revealed how interconnected leverage can cascade.

AGI-driven markets, operating at machine speed, could amplify such cascades if resilience is neglected.

Investors should prioritize:

- Firms building real-time risk monitoring
- Infrastructure that dampens volatility
- Cross-system interoperability safeguards
- Decentralized yet coordinated architectures

Resilience may appear conservative.

In reality, it is forward-looking.

The institutions that survive shocks become dominant in recovery phases.

Excellence is not avoiding volatility.

It is absorbing and adapting to it.

Aligning Incentives with Civilization-Scale Outcomes

AGI makes it technically feasible to measure outcomes beyond profit:

- Environmental impact
- Workforce development
- Community stability
- Long-term productivity growth

Investors who incorporate multidimensional optimization into mandates redefine success metrics.

This is not ideological.

It is strategic.

Capital that destabilizes its operating environment ultimately erodes its own returns.

Capital that strengthens its environment compounds sustainably.

The holy grail emerges when return generation and societal advancement reinforce each other rather than conflict.

The Role of Institutional Leadership

Large institutions, asset managers, global banks, and sovereign funds possess unique leverage.

They can:

- Influence regulatory frameworks
- Standardize ethical AI protocols
- Shape market infrastructure
- Direct capital into foundational layers

If they adopt purely short-term incentives, AGI will amplify speculative cycles.

If they adopt long-term excellence mandates, AGI can amplify coordination, inclusion, and innovation.

Leadership is not rhetorical.

It is structural.

What gets funded gets built.

What gets built defines the future market.

A Generational Opportunity

Moments of systemic transition occur rarely.

The telegraph reshaped trading.

Electronic exchanges reshaped speed.

Algorithmic finance reshaped execution.

AGI reshapes intelligence itself within capital markets.

Investors and leaders today are not merely selecting companies.

They are shaping the architecture of the next financial epoch.

Short-term gain will always exist.

But the opportunity to define excellence at system scale appears only once in a generation.

Closing Reflection: Choosing the Trajectory

If AGI becomes the nervous system of capital markets, then the values embedded in investment mandates will propagate through that nervous system.

Investors and leaders must ask:

- Are we amplifying concentration or expanding participation?
- Are we extracting value or creating new capacity?
- Are we optimizing for quarters or generations?
- Are we building fragility or resilience?

Excellence is not accidental.

It is steered.

The holy grail of capital markets in the AGI era is not merely superior return. It is a system where intelligence, capital, and inclusion align to elevate productivity and opportunity simultaneously.

Short-term gain may satisfy performance dashboards.

Long-term excellence shapes history.

And in an AGI amplified world, history will move faster than ever.

Those who think in decades and allocate accordingly will not only achieve returns.

They will define what success means in the age of intelligent capital.

ENTERPRISE READINESS: STRUCTURING THE ORGANIZATION FOR A SEAMLESS AGI TRANSITION

Technology transitions rarely fail because tools are unavailable.

They fail because organizations are unprepared.

As AGI begins reshaping capital markets, the greatest challenge for enterprises is not access to models; it is internal alignment. Strategy, governance, incentives, culture, infrastructure, and talent must evolve in synchrony. Without deliberate restructuring, AGI risks becoming fragmented experimentation rather than a systemic transformation.

This chapter explores how enterprises should begin structuring themselves organizationally and operationally to ensure a disciplined, resilient, and excellence-oriented transition to AGI.

Recognize That AGI Is Not an IT Upgrade

Many organizations will initially treat AGI as an extension of analytics or automation initiatives.

That is a mistake.

AGI affects:

- Decision-making authority
- Risk management frameworks
- Capital allocation processes
- Client engagement models
- Competitive positioning

It represents a strategic transformation rather than a technical deployment.

Enterprises must elevate AGI from a technology initiative to a board-level agenda.

If ownership remains siloed within IT departments, integration will remain shallow.

Establish a Central Intelligence Architecture

AGI deployments scattered across business units create fragmentation, redundancy, and risk.

Instead, enterprises should design a centralized intelligence architecture that:

- Standardizes model governance
- Ensures interoperability
- Maintains shared data integrity
- Provides enterprise-wide oversight

This does not mean centralizing all innovation.

It means centralizing standards while allowing decentralized experimentation within clear guardrails.

A coordinated intelligence backbone prevents shadow systems from proliferating.

Create a Dedicated AGI Governance Council

The transition to AGI touches compliance, risk, ethics, operations, HR, and strategy.

Enterprises should establish a cross-functional AGI governance council responsible for:

- Oversight of deployment priorities
- Ethical review of high-impact use cases
- Risk escalation protocols
- Regulatory alignment
- Strategic roadmap coordination

Without structured governance, innovation can outpace accountability.

Governance is not bureaucracy.

It is coherence.

Redesign Incentive Structures

Organizations optimize for what they reward.

If compensation structures prioritize short-term revenue, AGI initiatives will skew toward speculative gains rather than long-term excellence.

Enterprises must align incentives with:

- Sustainable value creation
- Risk-adjusted performance
- Inclusion expansion
- System resilience

Leaders should incorporate multi-year performance metrics into AGI-related projects.

AGI can amplify productivity, but without aligned incentives, it may also amplify short-termism.

Build an Internal AI-Literate Workforce

AGI cannot remain a black box accessible only to specialists.

Executives, risk officers, compliance teams, and front-line managers must understand:

- Model capabilities and limitations
- Bias risks
- Data dependencies
- Failure modes

This requires enterprise-wide AI literacy initiatives.

Training programs should focus not on coding but on:

- Decision interpretation
- Model validation
- Ethical implications
- Risk scenario planning

An organization that does not understand its own intelligence systems cannot manage them effectively.

Embed Explainability into Core Workflows

In capital markets, decisions must often be justified to regulators, clients, and internal oversight bodies.

Enterprises should design AGI systems with explain ability built in from the beginning.

That includes:

- Transparent decision logs

- Audit trails
- Model rationale summaries
- Human override mechanisms

Explain ability should not be retrofitted after deployment.

It must be part of the architectural design.

Trust becomes a competitive advantage.

Integrate Human Judgment with Autonomous Systems

The goal is not to eliminate human involvement.

It is to elevate it.

Enterprises should structure workflows so that:

- AGI handles pattern detection, optimization, and forecasting
- Humans focus on contextual judgment, ethical interpretation, and strategic decisions

This hybrid model requires a clear delineation of responsibilities.

Who overrides a model?

When does escalation occur?

How are conflicts resolved?

Ambiguity creates risk.

Clarity creates resilience.

Prioritize High-Impact, Low-Fragility Use Cases First

The temptation is to deploy AGI in high-return areas immediately.

But early deployments should focus on:

- Risk detection
- Fraud prevention
- Operational efficiency
- Compliance automation

These applications build internal confidence and institutional knowledge.

Speculative applications can be pursued once governance frameworks are mature.

A disciplined rollout reduces reputational and systemic risk.

Upgrade Risk Management for Machine-Speed Markets

AGI systems interacting across markets create new risk categories:

- Feedback loops
- Model correlation risk
- Autonomous decision cascades
- Data poisoning vulnerabilities

Risk teams must implement:

- Real-time monitoring tools
- Cross-model correlation tracking
- Continuous stress testing
- Incident response simulations

Traditional quarterly risk reviews are insufficient in environments operating at machine speed.

Risk oversight must evolve alongside intelligence deployment.

Protect Data as Strategic Infrastructure

Data becomes the fuel of AGI.

Enterprises must treat data governance as strategic infrastructure rather than administrative overhead.

This includes:

- Clean data pipelines
- Strong access controls
- Robust cybersecurity architecture
- Clear data lineage tracking

Poor data quality undermines model integrity.

Data integrity forms the foundation of institutional trust.

Collaborate With Regulators Early

Enterprises that proactively engage regulators gain a strategic advantage.

Instead of waiting for compliance mandates, organizations should:

- Share transparency frameworks
- Participate in regulatory sandboxes
- Contribute to standard-setting initiatives
- Offer insights on systemic implications

This reduces uncertainty and positions the enterprise as a trusted stakeholder.

Regulatory alignment minimizes long-term friction.

Invest in Resilience, Not Just Performance

Highly optimized AGI systems may generate impressive metrics until stressed.

Enterprises must build for resilience:

- Redundant systems
- Model fallback strategies
- Scenario simulations
- Crisis playbooks

Resilience protects both reputation and capital.

In volatile environments, stability becomes a premium.

Align AGI Strategy with Long-Term Vision

AGI initiatives should not exist as isolated experiments.

They must align directly with the enterprise mission.

Leaders should ask:

- How does AGI enhance our core value proposition?
- How does it improve client trust?
- How does it expand inclusion?
- How does it strengthen long-term competitiveness?

Without alignment, AGI remains tactical.

With alignment, it becomes transformative.

Cultivate a Culture of Responsible Innovation

Technology adoption often triggers cultural resistance.

Some fear displacement, while others fear loss of control.

Leadership must communicate clearly:

- AGI is augmentation, not replacement
- Ethical standards are non-negotiable

- Transparency is expected
- Continuous learning is valued

Culture determines whether a transformation succeeds.

A fearful organization resists innovation.

An aligned organization shapes it.

Phase the Transition Deliberately

A perfect transition does not mean instant adoption.

It requires a structured evolution:

Phase 1: Intelligence augmentation

Phase 2: Partial automation

Phase 3: Autonomous coordination with oversight

Phase 4: Adaptive enterprise architecture

Each phase should include evaluation, stress testing, and cultural integration.

Rushing increases fragility.

Measured scaling enhances stability.

Closing Reflection: Building the Intelligent Enterprise

The transition to AGI in capital markets is inevitable.

Excellence in that transition is not.

Enterprises must:

- Elevate AGI to a strategic priority
- Establish centralized governance while empowering decentralized innovation

- Align incentives with long-term value creation
- Invest in literacy, transparency, and resilience
- Integrate human judgment thoughtfully

The organizations that succeed will not be those with the most powerful models.

They will be those with the most coherent structure.

In an AGI-driven capital ecosystem, intelligence is accessible to many.

Leaders are differentiated by institutional excellence in governance, culture, resilience, and trust.

The perfect transition is not about speed.

It is about alignment.

Alignment, once achieved, compounds as powerfully as intelligence itself.

THE POLICYMAKER'S MANDATE: GUARDRAILS AGAINST RUNAWAY DISPARITY

Technological revolutions rarely fail because of a lack of intelligence.

They fail because of a lack of foresight.

As AGI integrates into capital markets, policymakers stand at a structural inflection point. The system shaped today will determine whether intelligent capital becomes a force for broad prosperity or a mechanism that accelerates concentration, fragility, and runaway inequality.

The danger is not hypothetical. Anyone paying attention to the market should recognize this by now.

When intelligence scales faster than governance, inequality compounds more rapidly than opportunity.

This chapter examines the role of policymakers: to identify the risk of runaway inequality early, to design incentive structures that promote inclusion, and to establish guardrails that prevent systemic imbalance before it spread.

Understanding Runaway Disparity in the AGI Capital Era

Runaway disparity is not ordinary inequality.

It is a self-reinforcing cycle in which:

- Advanced intelligence disproportionately benefits those who already possess capital and infrastructure
- Capital concentration increases access to superior models and data
- Superior models generate higher returns
- Higher returns further entrench dominance

In traditional markets, disparities widened gradually.

In AGI-driven systems, feedback loops operate at machine speed.

If left unchecked, advantages compound algorithmically.

This is not merely a social concern. It is a systemic risk.

Extreme concentration reduces competitive dynamism.

Reduced dynamism stifles innovation.

Stifled innovation erodes long-term growth.

Eroded growth destabilizes political and economic systems.

Runaway disparity is destabilizing for markets themselves.

Policymakers must recognize it early rather than reacting after structural damage becomes visible.

The Speed Problem

AGI compresses time.

Capital allocation decisions that once unfolded over months may now adjust in seconds. Risk spreads in milliseconds, and competitive advantages scale globally in weeks.

Policy frameworks, by contrast, move slowly.

If regulatory design lags behind technological acceleration, misalignment widens.

Policymakers must therefore:

- Anticipate structural shifts rather than responding only to crises
- Develop adaptive regulatory models
- Build continuous oversight mechanisms

The goal is not to slow innovation.

The goal is to ensure that innovation compounds broadly rather than concentrating narrowly.

Incentives Shape Systems

Markets optimize around incentives.

When short-term speculative returns are rewarded disproportionately, capital gravitates toward speculation.

When long-term productive investment is rewarded, capital gravitates toward creation.

Policymakers can influence these flows through:

- Tax structures
- Capital requirements
- Disclosure standards
- Subsidies and public-private partnerships
- Regulatory clarity for inclusive innovation

For example, if deploying AGI in underserved credit markets receives favorable regulatory treatment, innovation will flow there.

If building resilience infrastructure reduces compliance burdens, firms will prioritize stability systems.

Incentives act as the silent architects of market behavior.

Guardrails are necessary, yet incentives determine the direction.

Preventing Concentration of Intelligence Infrastructure

One of the greatest risks in the AGI-capital transition is the concentration of intelligence infrastructure.

If only a handful of actors control:

- Core AI models
- Data pipelines
- Risk analytics engines
- Clearing and coordination layers

market power becomes structurally embedded.

Policymakers must ensure:

- Competitive access to foundational AI infrastructure
- Interoperability standards
- Open auditing frameworks
- Anti-monopolistic oversight

Healthy competition is not merely about price; it is about innovation diversity.

Diverse intelligence systems reduce systemic correlation risk.

Concentration amplifies fragility.

Embedding Transparency and Auditability

AGI systems in capital markets will influence credit decisions, investment flows, insurance pricing, and risk management.

Opaque systems undermine trust.

Policymakers should require:

- Explainability standards for high-impact financial AI
- Independent auditing mechanisms
- Transparent data provenance requirements
- Clear accountability frameworks

Transparency does not hinder innovation.

It promotes trust.

Markets operate on confidence. When participants believe AI systems are biased, manipulative, or unaccountable, instability follows.

Guardrails preserve legitimacy.

Legitimacy ensures market continuity.

Designing for Inclusion at Scale

AGI enables granular personalization of financial services, creating an unprecedented opportunity to extend inclusion.

Policymakers can accelerate this by:

- Encouraging AI-based underwriting models that responsibly expand credit access
- Supporting digital identity infrastructure
- Incentivizing platforms that reduce transaction costs for small enterprises
- Promoting global interoperability for cross-border participation

Inclusion must not be an afterthought.

It must be embedded into regulatory architecture from the outset.

When participation broadens, growth becomes more robust.

Exclusion shrinks opportunity, while inclusion multiplies it.

Guarding Against Algorithmic Amplification of Bias

Even well-designed systems can inherit bias from data.

In capital markets, this bias can manifest as:

- Systematic under-allocation of capital
- Risk overpricing for specific communities
- Limited access to high-return investment opportunities

When these biases are encoded into AGI systems, they scale rapidly.

Policymakers must require:

- Bias detection and mitigation protocols
- Ongoing performance audits across demographic groups
- Clear remediation mechanisms

The objective is not artificial equalization.

It is fairness in access to opportunity.

A system that systematically excludes participants undermines its own long-term productive capacity.

Systemic Risk in a Machine-Speed Market

AGI agents interacting autonomously can create feedback loops that designers may not anticipate.

Flash crashes offered a preview.

Future cascades could be far more complex.

Policymakers must consider:

- Real-time supervisory technology (SupTech)
- AI-driven systemic risk monitoring
- Cross-institutional coordination frameworks
- Autonomous circuit breakers at the level of market infrastructure

The role of regulators evolves from periodic oversight to continuous engagement.

Guardrails must function at machine speed whenever markets operate at machine speed.

Aligning Public and Private Incentives

Governments cannot construct the entire future market architecture on their own.

However, they can influence its shape.

Public-private collaboration should focus on:

- Establishing shared standards for ethical AI in finance
- Creating data-sharing frameworks that protect privacy while enabling innovation
- Developing sandboxes to safely test new financial models
- Making joint investments in foundational infrastructure

The goal is alignment.

When private capital perceives clarity and stability in regulatory direction, it invests with confidence.

When policy is uncertain or reactive, investment either hesitates or concentrates defensively.

Measuring What Matters

Policymakers often rely on lagging indicators such as GDP growth, unemployment rates, and inflation metrics.

In an AGI-enhanced capital market, additional indicators become critical:

- Capital concentration ratios
- Distribution metrics for AI access
- Inclusion growth rates
- Real-time systemic correlation measures

To prevent runaway disparity, policymakers must track structural signals early.

Measurement precedes management.

If disparity compounds unnoticed, intervention becomes costly and disruptive.

When detected early, subtle incentive adjustments can redirect capital flows effectively.

The Cost of Inaction

Failure to establish guardrails carries serious consequences:

- Accelerated wealth concentration
- Reduced social mobility
- Political instability
- Erosion of institutional trust
- Cycles of regulatory backlash

Markets perform best in stable environments.

If disparity reaches extreme levels, policy responses may become abrupt and heavy-handed, further destabilizing markets.

Proactive governance prevents reactive disruption.

The cost of thoughtful early intervention is far lower than the cost of correcting systemic failures.

Excellence as a Policy Objective

Policymakers should not focus solely on preventing harm.

They should focus on enabling excellence.

Excellence in the AGI-driven capital era includes:

- Broad participation
- Dynamic innovation
- Stable risk frameworks
- Transparent systems
- Alignment between private returns and public benefit

Guardrails prevent collapse.

Incentives enable growth and flourishing.

Both elements are essential.

Closing Reflection: Stewardship of an Intelligent System

AGI will not replace policymakers.

However, it will amplify the consequences of their decisions.

In an intelligent capital system, the values encoded in regulation become part of the operating logic of markets.

Policymakers must recognize that the danger of runaway disparity is not merely a moral concern but a structural economic risk.

They must:

- Design incentives that reward inclusion
- Enforce transparency and competition
- Monitor systemic interactions
- Align innovation with long-term stability

If entrepreneurs build the tools and investors steer the capital, policymakers define the boundaries.

Boundaries determine whether intelligence expands opportunity or concentrates it.

The holy grail of the AGI-driven capital market era is not just efficiency.

It is a system in which innovation, inclusion, and resilience reinforce each other.

Guardrails make this possible.

Without them, intelligence can accelerate disparity.

With them, intelligence can elevate an entire civilization.

A defining opportunity of this kind is now on the horizon.

AT THE EDGE OF INTELLIGENCE: A CHOICE THAT WILL DEFINE US

There are moments in history when humanity stands quietly at the edge of something immense.

Not a war.

Not a collapse.

Not a visible crisis.

But a shift.

The integration of Artificial General Intelligence (AGI) into capital markets is one of those moments. It does not arrive with smoke or sirens. It arrives through code, through systems, and through subtle shifts in how decisions are made, how capital moves, how risk is priced, and how opportunity is distributed.

And yet its consequences may echo for generations.

We are not merely upgrading technology.

We are rewriting the nervous system of economic civilization.

Capital markets are not abstract charts and tickers. They are the circulatory system of human possibility. They determine which ideas come alive, which communities rise, which technologies scale, and which dreams receive oxygen.

When intelligence becomes embedded in that system, when algorithms begin to guide allocation, and when models optimize flows at machine speed, the values we encode into those systems will begin to compound.

And that is where the real choice begins.

Entrepreneurs will build the new architecture. They will create platforms that can analyze, allocate, coordinate, and optimize with a precision never before possible. But they must ask themselves a question that goes deeper than valuation and speed:

Are we building engines of extraction, or engines of elevation?

It is easy to chase inefficiencies. It is easy to build tools that capture fleeting advantage. But there is a higher calling, which is to design systems that markets will rely on, trust, and grow with. To build not just for disruption, but for durability. Not just for performance, but for fairness. Not just for dominance, but for participation.

The entrepreneurs who shape this era will not be remembered only for their technical brilliance. They will be remembered for what they chose to amplify.

Investors and leaders hold a different kind of power, quieter but perhaps more decisive.

They steer.

Capital flows where incentives point. If the compass is set toward short-term extraction, intelligence will magnify speculation. If it is set toward long-term creation, intelligence will magnify productivity.

It is always tempting to measure success by the next quarter. But AGI does not operate on quarterly horizons. It compounds. It scales. It accelerates feedback loops.

The question leaders must confront is deeply human:

What future are we financing?

Are we funding systems that narrow opportunity into the hands of the few, or systems that expand participation to the many? Are we rewarding fragility masked as efficiency, or resilience built with foresight?

The holy grail of intelligent capital is not simply higher returns. It is alignment, where financial gain and societal progress reinforce one another rather than compete.

When capital is steered wisely, it does not merely accumulate. It cultivates.

Enterprises, too, stand at a threshold.

Organizations built over decades must now integrate intelligence that learns, adapts, and evolves faster than any previous system. This is not an IT upgrade. It is a cultural transformation.

Companies must decide whether intelligence will remain a siloed experiment or become an integrated force guided by ethics, governance, and purpose.

An enterprise that adopts AGI recklessly may move quickly, but it will move blindly. An enterprise that adopts it with care, transparency, and accountability will move with confidence.

The intelligent enterprise is not defined by the power of its models. It is defined by the clarity of its mission and the integrity of its structure.

In this transition, structure is destiny.

And then there are policymakers, the often unseen architects of boundaries.

They do not build platforms or allocate venture rounds. But they shape incentives. They protect trust. They guard against imbalance before it spirals into instability.

Runaway disparity is not an abstract fear. In an AGI-accelerated world, concentration can compound faster than correction. Advantages can scale before society has time to respond.

Policymakers must look beyond today's metrics and anticipate tomorrow's dynamics. They must design systems that encourage inclusion, preserve competition, and embed transparency. They must ensure that intelligence, once unleashed, does not become a force that narrows opportunity or destabilizes markets.

Guardrails are not restrictions on progress.

They are conditions for sustainable progress.

Without them, acceleration can fracture society.

With them, acceleration can elevate it.

The truth is this: none of these actors operates in isolation.

Entrepreneurs shape tools.

Investors shape direction.

Enterprises shape execution.

Policymakers shape boundaries.

Together, they shape trajectory. And trajectory, once set in a self-reinforcing system, becomes difficult to reverse.

That is why anticipation matters.

The danger is not that AGI will arrive, it will.

The danger is that we drift into its consequences without intention.

History teaches that technology magnifies the values of its era. If short-termism dominates, technology amplifies it. If foresight guides, technology amplifies that instead.

We cannot afford to sleepwalk through this transition. Because once intelligence governs allocation at scale, the patterns it reinforces will ripple through employment, innovation, wealth distribution, and opportunity itself.

This is not simply about markets.

It is about the architecture of civilization.

There are two paths before us.

One path leads to concentration, where intelligence accelerates advantage for those already positioned to benefit. Where optimization outruns fairness. Where efficiency overshadows resilience. Where disparity compounds quietly until it fractures trust.

The other path leads to excellence, where intelligence broadens access, stabilizes risk, unlocks dormant productivity, and aligns capital with long-term flourishing. Where innovation is guided by inclusion. Where resilience is valued alongside performance. Where growth is shared and therefore sustainable.

Neither path is guaranteed.

The difference lies in decisions made now: in boardrooms, in startup labs, in investment committees, in regulatory chambers.

Excellence does not emerge automatically from intelligent systems.

It emerges from intelligent choices.

This is a rare moment.

Few generations are given the responsibility of redesigning the foundational systems of their economy. Fewer still are given the tools to do so with unprecedented intelligence.

AGI offers power.

But power without direction magnifies instability.

Power with wisdom magnifies progress.

The question before us is not whether markets will become intelligent.

They will.

The question is whether we will become wise enough to guide them.

If we choose long-term thinking over short-term gain, inclusion over concentration, resilience over fragility, and trust over opacity, then the integration of AGI into capital markets can become one of the great elevating chapters of human history.

Not because the technology was extraordinary.

But because the decisions were.

And in the end, it is not intelligence alone that defines an era.

It is the values we choose to encode within it.

To the disruptors and the driven: the spark is in your hands.
Will you start the fire?

ABOUT THE AUTHOR

Chidananda "Chida" Khatua is a technology leader, entrepreneur, and expert in artificial intelligence whose work sits at the intersection of innovation, business, and human impact. Chida is **CEO and founder** of **Temporal Dynamics** and **Chairman and founder of QuantumStreet AI**, he has steered the company at the forefront of applying machine learning to real-world decision-making, building scalable AI systems that bridge research and industry. Prior to founding Quantum Street, Chida spent nearly two decades shaping advanced technology **at Intel** and launching his own successful startup, demonstrating both technical depth and entrepreneurial vision. His contributions span **multiple patents** in hardware, software, and AI technologies. Recognized by *Business Insider* as one of the "Top 10 People Transforming Investing" and among the "Top 100 People Transforming Business" Chida combines leadership with a commitment to ethical and impactful innovation. He holds advanced degrees from **Stanford University**, the **Indian Institute of Science**, **University College of Engineering**, and an **MBA from the Haas School of Business at the University of California,**

Berkeley a blend of technical rigor and strategic insight that informs his writing and thought leadership on technology, society, and the future of intelligence.

https://www.linnkedin.com/in/chida

Made in the USA
Coppell, TX
06 June 2026

79112346R00111